THE PROBLEM OF NATIONAL EDUCATION IN INDIA

THE PROBLEM OF NATIONAL EDUCATION IN INDIA

BY

LAJPAT RAI

GYAN

Published by

GYAN

Gyan Publishing House
5, Ansari Road
Daryaganj, New Delhi-110002
Phone: 011-47034999, 9811692060
E-mail: books@gyanbooks.com

Distribution Network
gyanbooks.com
India, USA, Canada, UK, Australia, France

ISBN: 978-81-212-7969-7 (PB)
First Published, 1920

2nd Impression 2023

Printed at: Gyan Press, Delhi.

THE PROBLEM OF NATIONAL EDUCATION IN INDIA
Author: LAJPAT RAI

THE PROBLEM OF NATIONAL EDUCATION IN INDIA

BOOKS BY THE SAME AUTHOR

YOUNG INDIA. B. W. Huebsch, New York

ENGLAND'S DEBT TO INDIA. B. W. Huebsch, New York

AN OPEN LETTER TO LLOYD GEORGE. B. W. Huebsch, New York

THE POLITICAL FUTURE OF INDIA. B. W. Huebsch, New York.

AN OPEN LETTER TO EDWIN SAMUEL MONTAGU

REFLECTIONS ON THE POLITICAL SITUATION IN INDIA

THE EVOLUTION OF JAPAN, and Other Essays.

THE UNITED STATES: A Hindu Study.

THE ARYA SAMAJ.

THE PROBLEM OF NATIONAL EDUCATION IN INDIA

BY

LAJPAT RAI

LONDON: GEORGE ALLEN & UNWIN LTD.
RUSKIN HOUSE, 40 MUSEUM STREET, W.C. 1

DEDICATED

TO

MY FATHER

PREFACE

THIS book has grown in greater volume than I intended. It is still incomplete. I would have liked to have added a few more chapters, for example, on the value and method of teaching music, on the value and method of teaching social subjects, and so on. I feel, however, that these topics must be reserved for treatment in a subsequent volume. The urgency of the question demands the immediate publication of these articles in book form. The book does not claim to provide anything new for experts or for those who have made a special study of education as a science. It is meant for the lay reader. Its object is to educate the people in the problem of education in India and to help in the formation of public opinion.

A few more words about my right to claim a hearing on the subject. In the first place I have the honour of being the son of a teacher—the first of a group trained by the British Government in its normal schools in the 'sixties. My father stood at the top of his class, securing in some subjects the highest marks given. I received my first training from him. Excepting English, I learnt practically everything else from him until I passed my middle school examination and joined the High School at Lahore. I owe to him my interest in education. I have met numerous teachers in my life, but in India I have never come across a better teacher than he. He treated his pupils like comrades and enjoyed their company. He gave the best in him to his pupils, not in a spirit of giving, but in a spirit of co-operation. Wherever he went he was the idol of his pupils. He never cared how much they remembered of the text, so long as they had an intelligent grasp of the subject he taught. He never taught; he just helped them learn in their own way. All this was natural to him, since, not knowing a word of the English language, he never studied the science nor the art (whatever you wish to call it) of teaching. In the second place, ever since I left school I have been actively associated with educational movements. My educational activities are known to my countrymen, and I need not mention them in detail. The study of educational institutions, educational ideals, and educational methods has been one of the passions of my life. In foreign countries also I have devoted a substantial part of my time and energy to the study of educational questions, always with a view to their adaptation to the needs of India. This book is the result of these studies.

The work was written in the second half of 1918, while the war was still going on. It was ready for the press in the beginning of 1919, but publication was delayed on account of the absence of the author from England.

LAJPAT RAI.

NEW YORK, U.S.A.
January, 1920.

CONTENTS

CONTENTS

The Problem of National Education in India

I

NATIONAL EDUCATION

INTRODUCTORY

A

THE Indian papers at hand report that our publicists are engaged in a discussion of the question of "national education" for India. The movement, led by some of the sincerest and most devoted leaders of the nationalist movement for Home Rule for India, appears to be spreading. From the stray papers that I have received, I have not been able to find out the exact position of those who are reported to have struck a note of mild dissent, more by way of criticism than of opposition, but they give some idea of the position of those who are supporting the movement. Mrs. Besant has kindly mentioned my name as one of those who pioneered the movement in the Punjab, in the eighties of the last century. It is quite true that I am one of those persons who raised the cry of "national education" in North India, so far back as 1883, and I have since then used it rather effectively for enlisting sympathy and collecting funds for the various institutions that were from time to time started to impart education on "nationalist" lines. It is also obvious that the nationalism that we preached in those days was rather narrow and sectarian. Sir Syed Ahmad Khan was the first among the leaders of thought in North India who set afloat the idea of denominational education. The Christian institutions had led the way before him. The Mohammedan Anglo-Oriental College at Aligarh was a symbol of the new Muslim nationalism which Sir Syed Ahmad Khan founded, educational in function, but political in scope and effect.

The Arya Samaj, representing the new nationalism of the Hindus, followed suit, and the Dayananda Anglo-Vedic College, at Lahore, was the fruit of its efforts. Then came the movement of the Central Hindu College at Benares, upon which has now been erected the superstructure of the Hindu

University. The Mohammedan College at Aligarh, the Arya College at Lahore, the Hindu College at Benares, all embodied the "national" ideals of their founders, limited and sectarian as they were at the time. Each professed to provide its own kind of national education. The educational facilities provided by these institutions were open to persons of all creeds, denominations and religions, but the nationalism aimed at was undisguisedly denominational. Each institution created an atmosphere of its own —national to a certain extent, so far as the general cult of love of country was concerned, but otherwise openly sectarian.

The education imparted in these institutions, as distinguished from the ordinary state-owned schools and colleges, was "national" only in so far as it helped the creation of the denominational atmosphere aimed at by its promulgators. The Muslim College and the Hindu Colleges all professed to enforce and encourage the study of the vernaculars and their sacred languages, but the emphasis all the time was on the University course and the University examinations. The scheme of studies promulgated by the official Universities was accepted unreservedly, except in the additions that were made to the courses in Hindi and Urdu, Sanskrit and Arabic. The principal business of the staffs engaged was to prepare students for University examinations. The results achieved in these examinations were the measure of their success and popularity. In the two colleges in the United Provinces, the leading positions on the staff were reserved for Europeans. Special efforts were no doubt made in each institution to inoculate the students with the serum of that narrow nationalism which had inspired its founders. Subscriptions were raised and endowments made for the dissemination of religion, for the encouragement of the study of Sanskrit, Arabic and Persian. Some attempts were also made to encourage original research in the literatures and records that existed in these languages, with a view to propping up the several interpretations that the founders and the managers put upon their respective religions and their histories ; but the success achieved in this line was in each case dubious and almost imperceptible.

I am speaking more definitely of the Dayananda Anglo-Vedic College at Lahore, with the management of which I was intimately associated for about a quarter of a century. For over nine years I was the general secretary of the governing body, and for several years its Vice-President. I hope I shall not be charged with vanity if I say that for twenty-five years I gave the best in me to the institution—grudged neither time nor money nor energy in doing all that I could to ensure its success and progress. My duties were by no means confined to field and office work (running the office, addressing public meetings, collecting subscriptions, doing publicity work, conducting and writing for periodicals, etc.), but included close association with the staff and the students, and the supervision of the different departments, particularly the boarding houses.

It is with immense pleasure and pride that I look back upon that period of my life. It was a rare privilege to associate and co-operate with men of the character and calibre of Hansraj, Lal Chand, Dwarka Dass, Ishwar Dass, and others, too numerous to be mentioned here. Their spirit was denominational and sectarian, no doubt, but there was hardly anything of meanness, or pettiness, or jealousy in it. Even their sectarianism was of an exalted kind; the Country, the Motherland, always had the uppermost place in their affections.

They were all inspired by a spirit of genuine and disinterested patriotism and altruism. Their methods were clean and above-board. It was a joy to work with them.

Of all the schemes of national education promulgated till then, theirs was probably the first which took cognizance of the economic problem. They were probably the first to include in their educational programme the idea of "Swadeshi." The original prospectus of the Dayananda Anglo-Vedic College was remarkable for these things : (*a*) the emphasis it laid on bridging the gulf between the educated classes and the uneducated masses ; (*b*) the emphasis on the necessity of technical education in arts and industries, which would make the future leaders of the country independent of State service, and (*c*) an insistence that their scheme of national education be absolutely independent of Government patronage and Government help.

Looking back at the record of the institution for the last thirty-two years of its life, giving all possible credit to the founder and the managers and the leaders thereof for the best intentions and the best efforts, I regret to say that failure in their principal aims, expressed and unexpressed, is writ large on it. Let me guard against misunderstanding. There is no man in India for whom I have greater respect than Hansraj, the founder President of the Arya College, nor another body of men in the whole country towards whom I entertain feelings of greater respect, regard, and reverence than the past and present bodies of the Dayananda College. The spirit of self-sacrifice and national service shown by Hansraj and his pupils is almost unique, and worthy of the highest praise. The work done by them deserves all credit. The tiny bark of high education in the Punjab was rescued by this college at a time of its greatest danger. The spirit of public service in the land of the five rivers owes an immeasurable debt to the little band of workers who brought the college into existence and have run it since. Considering the positions and the resources of the men who conceived the idea and worked hard to make it a success, considering the general air of all-round suspicion and distrust in which they lived and worked, the story of the financial and educational success of the Dayananda Anglo-Vedic College, Lahore, is nothing short of a romance.

The Muslim College at Aligarh and the

Hindu College at Benares were both started under better auspices, blessed with the smiles of the leading aristocracy of their respective communities, and with the goodwill of the ruling authorities. The Arya College had none of these advantages. It was founded, managed, and run for a long time in defiance of both. Every brick of this institution has its own story which, perhaps, will never see the light of day. These stories have already been forgotten, and the few that are current will be burned with the bodies of those who composed them, not in words, but in deeds. Yes, all this is true; it is a pleasure and a privilege to be able to say this. Yet it must be owned that in solving the problems of national education, the Arya College at Lahore has been as conspicuous a failure as the other institutions started with similar objects in other parts of the country. Prior to the foundation of the National College in Bengal, the Dayananda Anglo-Vedic College at Lahore was the only institution in the country which could, even by a stretch of imagination and language, lay any claim to being called "national" in the sense in which the word was understood then. The Fergusson College is named after a foreigner, and with the exception of the spirit of self-sacrifice of its founder, directors, and teachers, had no other claim to be distinguished from the ordinary State Colleges. Both the Aligarh College and the Benares College have constantly had foreigners on their staffs, and have, besides, in common with the Fergusson College at Poona, been almost regularly in receipt of State aid, thus subjecting practically the whole of their policy to Government control. Not that that fact necessarily makes them denationalized, but it does reduce their claim to any great distinction from the ordinary State-managed institutions.

Besides the institutions mentioned above, there are some others also which claim to impart national education and which have been founded for that purpose. One of them is the Gurukula academy at Hardwar, founded by Munshi Rama and his party. The Gurukula, too, is a sectarian institution. Otherwise it certainly has a greater claim to being "national" than any of the others mentioned previously. It is an institution founded, managed, staffed, and financed by Indians only. In its curriculum it gives the first place to Indian languages. It is more in conformity with the spirit of

Hinduism than the College at Lahore, or the Central Hindu College at Benares. It takes no notice of the official University courses or the University examinations. It enforces a discipline which is more truly national than anything done in the other institutions. All that has been said about the spirit of self-sacrifice of those who founded the Dayananda Anglo-Vedic College is applicable to it. Yet I am afraid it is no more national than any of the others.

Another institution of almost the same kind is the Tagore School at Bolpur. It does not profess to impart high education, and is a one-man institution. There may be some other institutions which claim to cater to national education, with whose origin and history I am not acquainted. If so, I beg to be pardoned for not noticing them. It is not my purpose to give a complete list of "national" schools and colleges. The object is to review some typical efforts.

The only effort of this kind which was, in my judgment, truly national, was that made by the National Council of Education in Bengal, under the impetus of the Swadeshi and the Boycott. The scheme of the National Council was free from the sectarian tinge of the Upper India movements; it took no notice of denominational nationalism; it took ample cognizance of the economic needs of the country as a whole, and it frankly recognized the necessity of ignoring the official University curriculum on the one hand and State aid on the other. It aimed at national consolidation and national independence. It was a direct challenge to the Government, and the Government accepted it whole-heartedly. What came of it is known to everybody, and need not be stated here. It failed, as it was bound to do, because it came into conflict with the State.

The National Council of Education still exists, but only in name. Its condition is moribund. The leaders and officers themselves have strangulated it. Mr. T. Palit and Sir Rash Behari Ghosh, two of its strongest pillars, gave it a death-blow when they handed over their magnificent endowment to the Calcutta University, instead of to the National Council of Education, founded and led by them. The few scholars who, with characteristic self-sacrifice, gave up careers to give instruction to the students of the National College, are all dispersed. They are seeking appointments in Government-aided institutions. The Nationalist schools, started by the Council, have, most of them, been disintegrated by the force of circumstances, and at the present moment the movement is nothing but a dilapidated and discarded landmark in the educational progress of the country.

The only institutions that are still in existence and prospering are the denominational ones. The Dayananda Anglo-Vedic College at Lahore and the Mohammedan Anglo-Oriental College at Aligarh are thriving and a source of joy to their founders. They follow the policy of least or no resistance. The Dayananda Anglo-Vedic College, which was under suspicion ever since its birth, has more or less gained the confidence of the rulers by a radical change in its policy, and the reins of the Mohammedan College at Aligarh are held tightly by the Government. The Benares College is an independent University which enjoys both the confidence and the control of the Government. The Gurukula at Kangri is virtually the only institution that is really independent of Government control. It was under a cloud for a long time, until Sir James Meston and Lord Hardinge put upon it the seal of their approbation. I think the same might be said of Tagore's school at Bolpur.

Now I do not mean to insinuate even by implication that these institutions have not been educationally useful to the nation, or that their managers or leaders were not actuated by the best of motives. The remarks that I have made above about the Arya Samaj institutions apply, with equal force, to almost all these institutions. They are, without exception, monuments to the *patriotism* and public spirit of their founders and managers, and far be it from me to make any reflection on them.

Yet I cannot help repeating once more that they have not, except by their failure, made any substantial contribution toward the solution of the problem of "national" education. I want the leaders of the new movement to realize that fully, and to keep it in mind in formulating their new scheme. I, for one, do not believe in living in a fool's paradise. The first thing is to clear our minds of cant and have a clear conception of what we mean by national education.

B

I have before me three pronouncements on "national education"; one by Mrs. Annie Besant, the other by Mr. B. G. Tilak, and the third by Sir Rash Behari Ghosh. Of these, Mrs. Besant's is perhaps the only one which embodies ideas on the subject. I say this without any disrespect to the others. I will, therefore, consider that one first.

Says Mrs. Besant :—

> Nothing can more swiftly emasculate national life, nothing can more surely weaken national character, than allowing the education of the young to be controlled by foreign influences, to be dominated by foreign ideals. From 1896, onwards, I have ventured to urge on the Indian people that the education which was given to their sons was denationalizing and despiritualizing. Foreign habits, foreign manners, foreign dress, foreign ways are all enforced in a foreign language, with, in missionary schools, a foreign religion to boot, sterilizing the boy's heart, and despiritualizing his whole nature. Is it any wonder that the national spirit decayed, until a vigorous effort was made to capture education by . . .

Coming to the constructive side of the problem, Mrs. Besant propounds the question "What must our national education be ?" and then answers it in the following terms :—

> (1) It must be controlled by Indians, shaped by Indians, carried on by Indians. *It must hold up Indian ideals of devotion, wisdom and morality, and must be permeated by the Indian religious spirit* rather

than fed on the letter of the creeds. That spirit is spacious, tolerant, all-embracing, and recognizes that man goes to God along many roads and that all the prophets came from him.

(2) National education must live in an atmosphere of proud and glorious patriotism, and this atmosphere must be kept sweet, fresh, and bracing by the study of Indian literature, Indian history, Indian triumphs in science, in art, in politics, in war, in colonization, in manufactures, in trade, in commerce. The Arthashastra must be studied as well as the Dharmashastra, science and politics as well as religion.

(3) National education must not be separated from the homes of the nation. The ideals, the interests, the principles, the emotions of the one must be those of the other. For the nation is built out of families, and the present opposition between the home and the school must cease. The teachers in school and college must work in harmony with the teachers in the home.

(4) National education must meet the national temperament at every point, and develop the national character. India is not to become a lesser—nor even a greater—England, but to evolve into a mightier India. British ideals are good for Britain, but it is India's ideals that are good for India. We do not want echoes nor monotones; we want a choral melody of nations, mirroring the varied qualities of Nature and of God. Shall Nature show but a single colour, and trees, and flowers, and mountains, and sky wear but a single hue? Harmonious variety and not monotony is the mark of perfection.

Away from all apologies for India, with all deprecatory explanations of India's ways and customs, and traditions. India is herself, and needs not to be justified; *for verily, God has evolved no greater, no more exquisite nationality than India's among all the broken reflections of His own perfect beauty.*

The language of this pronouncement is dear to the heart of every nationalist. It is spirited and stimulating as well as ennobling and encouraging. As a piece of rhetoric, it is exquisite. I have often used similar language, and with good results. I may use it again if occasion demands it. We Indians owe a great debt of gratitude to Mrs. Besant for her activities in connection with the Theosophical Society and the Central Hindu College at Benares. Our obligations to her have grown immensely, both in volume and intensity, by her lead and interest in the Home Rule movement. Consequently, anything that comes from her must receive our careful and respectful consideration. Yet these facts make it all the more incumbent upon us not to hesitate to say "we differ," when, after a careful and respectful consideration,. we do differ from her. I am certain that she does not want us to follow her blindly. She lays no claim to infallibility.

Indian publicists have a duty to perform. They are planning the future of their nation, which is at the present moment in a state of transition and is undergoing a process of transformation. So much depends on education. Education is *the* vital question for us. It is the most important of all our problems. In a way it is the fundamental problem. We cannot afford to have loose and confused ideas about education, the aims and ends of education, and the methods of education. Our whole future hinges on it. It behoves us, therefore, to devote all the mental energy which we possess to the right understanding and the right solution thereof. It would not do to be carried away by prejudices and mere sentimentality. The decision must be arrived at by deep, careful and critical consideration of the whole question. A hastily arrived at decision, or one that is founded on prejudice and sentimentality, may materially hinder our progress or, at any rate, slow down the rate of progress.

The national mind is just now in a fluid condition. It needs wise and thoughtful guidance. Like wax, it will take such impressions as those whom the people love and respect, and in whose wise leadership they have confidence, will give. Tendencies created, prejudices reared, sentiments disseminated, where they go deep into the psychology of the nation, are difficult to be uprooted. To create national tendencies, sentiments, prejudices, impressions, and preferments in haste, under the idea that they can be corrected, later, when found to be wrong, involves so much waste of energy and opportunity that no wise leader ought to do it light-heartedly. This essay is only a plea for careful, critical consideration, as well as broad, thoughtful planning. There is no intention to indulge in petty or destructive criticism, nor to pose as an oracle.

II

NATIONAL IDEALS

FIRST we should come to a clear understanding of what our national ideals consist. Do we want to be part of the "civilized world," making our contribution to its progress, by thought and action, or do we want to be an isolated national unit, happy in our retirement and isolation? Of course we want political liberty, economic independence, social solidarity and religious freedom, but for what end? Are these things ends in themselves or only means to some other and higher end? If so, what is it?

Some will say that salvation is the ultimate end we desire. But what is meant by "salvation"? Is it the *nirvána* of Buddhism, the merging of the individual soul in the supreme soul of the *vedanta*, the temporary bliss of the Arya Samaj, the *mukti* of the Christian, or the paradise of the orthodox Moslem? Or are these, after all, only delusions? The real salvation lies in freedom from misery, poverty, disease, ignorance and slavery of every kind, in this life, now and here for ourselves and hereafter for our successors. There are religions which enjoin on their followers the duty of suffering all the pangs of misery, poverty, disease, ignorance and slavery, in order to have the certainty of bliss and happiness in the life to come. In fact, this is more or less the tendency of all religions which have been systematized.

From the earnestness which all classes of Indians are displaying in fighting misery, poverty, disease, ignorance, and slavery, it appears that they have made up their minds on one question at least: whatever the ultimate salvation may be, *mukti* or *nijat* or *nirvána*, our people do not want misery, poverty, disease, ignorance and slavery either for themselves or for their children. Hindus (Sanatanists, Arya Samajists, Brahmo Samajists, Vedantists and others), Moslems, Christians, all are agreed on this point. Every one is trying to explain his own dogma or creed in such a way as to make a pursuit of happiness in this world, by the righteous acquisition of wealth and health and knowledge, a desirable end. The natural bent of the human mind is also in the same direction.

But priests, prophets and reformers are not dead, nor do they show any signs of death. They are just hiding their heads and biding their time. With the least encouragement and stimulus they come out into the open and start their poisonous propaganda. *Vairaga*, a life of renunciation and poverty, is still the ostensible goal of every religion. *Sannyasis*, *dervishes* and monks are still our ideals of men. Even the most rational and liberal minded reformer respects and reveres them. Men of religion we call them ; and hence our instinctive, impulsive, deep-rooted sentiment is in their favour. What is worse, some modern and educated men, who are neither priests nor monks, and who, in most cases, do not themselves lead a life of asceticism, are holding up that ideal for their younger countrymen.

Every religion contains beautiful and sublime principles which save its followers from utter annihilation in the struggle for life, be it individual or social, but the bulk of every religious teaching and its literature as ordinarily understood lays emphasis on the *negation* of life, as distinguished from its assertion and intensification.

Higher Hindu religion teaches that salvation lies in *gnán* (knowledge), not mere knowledge, but realized knowledge. It insists that those who aspire to this kind of knowledge must live a full life, albeit a controlled life, before they can acquire that kind of *gnán.* They must do their full duty to society and learn all that has to be learnt by social amenities, relations and sensations. Then they can renounce certain phases of life, in favour of certain others. A vow of poverty did not in ancient times involve an exaltation of poverty over wealth, but only freedom from the obligations of property at a certain stage of one's life. In fact, the most ancient literature of the Hindus makes no mention, except by far-fetched implication, of Sannyasis. All the great Rishis and Munis of the past had property, as well as families. They preferred to live away from crowds only for purposes of research, for *yoga Samádhi* and concentration of mind on the problems of life. That condition was not an end in itself, but a new social means for a social end.

It was not a desire of *mukti* that led them to do it, but the very social and admirable desire of helping humanity by a rational solution of the problems of life. Look how this ideal was degraded in later times, until we came to exalt a life of mere *tyag* (renunciation) as such, and to place it at the top of life's edifice as a goal, an end, and a lighthouse. It is true the whole nation never practised it, but that was because it was impossible to do so. As many people as wished to adopt it did adopt it, until we find that to-day a good part of the nation (sometimes estimated at one-fourth), having abandoned all productive economic work, engages itself in preaching the virtues of *vairága* (asceticism) and in making the people believe that next to becoming a Sadhú himself, the best thing for a man to do to avoid damnation is to feed and maintain Sadhús.

I am afraid what I have said of Hinduism is also more or less true of Mohammedanism and of Christianity. So deep-rooted is the sentiment that iconoclastic reforming agencies like the Arya Samaj, the Brahmo Samaj and the Vivekananda Mission among the Hindus often drift in the same direction. Their hymns and songs and prayers are still brimful of that spirit. At the time when English education began to be imported into India, this fatal tendency towards the negation of life was a substantial part of the *national* character. We may defend our respective religions against the charge of having taught this negation, but we cannot with any honesty deny the fact of the prevalence of this spirit to an alarming extent among our people. Nor can we conceal that, more or less, the whole of our literature is full of this tendency. We may call them additions of degenerate times, but there they are. No one reading that literature can evade the subtle influence of this all-pervading tendency. Our Epics are the most human documents we possess. Yet even they are full of that spirit.

Now it must be owned that the present awakening, the protest against this tendency, owes its birth to foreign education, however godless it may have been. Sometimes I feel thankful for its very godlessness. But for this education there might have been no awakening, or to be more accurate, the awakening might have been indefinitely delayed. To my mind the first need of India is the absolute destruction of this tendency towards the negation of life. It is the fundamental basis of our whole national weakness. Christianity too has this tendency, but if the Christian nations had adhered to true Christianity, they would have made no progress at all. It is not Christianity that has produced the modern improvements in life. Progress in Europe has been made in spite of Christianity. The most important work before us then is to change the general psychology of our people in this respect; to create in them an interest, a zest for real life.

The general prevailing idea of life in India is that it is a necessary evil. That life itself is a misery and a misfortune from which it is desirable to escape, is so deeply written in the souls of our people, that it is not easy to efface it. What India needs is an earnest, widely spread, persistent effort to teach and preach the gospel of life. That life is real, precious, earnest, invaluable, to be prized, preserved, prolonged and enjoyed, is not so obvious to our people as it should be. Not that the Indians do not value living; not that they have no respect for life as such; nay, in fact some of them care for mere life so much, as to preserve inferior lives even at the sacrifice or the detriment of human life. The vast bulk of them prefer mere living to honourable living.

The ancient Hindus seem to have had a clear idea of the amount of energy that had been expended by the race in the evolution of man. The idea is so deep-rooted that every Hindu rustic will tell you what a privilege it is to be born a human being. So far he is all right. The trouble begins when he starts to consider the aim of life. As to that he is being told day in and day out that supreme merit lies in killing desire, in escaping from the life of the senses so as to escape from the pain of rebirth. This necessarily leads him to shun life, to belittle it, and eventually to escape from it if he can. I admit that this is a perversion of the original doctrine, and that there is not sufficient sanction for it in the ancient scripture, but then that is the prevailing belief which finds ample support and justification from the language of the sacred books.

The first aim of a national system of education should be to destroy this belief. This cannot be achieved by a promulgation and perpetuation of that literature in its present form, which is over full with this false view of life's aim. Personally I have a great affection for the Sanskrit language and the literature contained in it, but in my judgment any attempt to make it a medium of general education and uplift is bound to fail and deserves to fail.

Its value for the purposes of historic research is obvious. Its aid to enrich the vocabulary of our vernaculars is indispensable. Its cultivation for purposes of scholarship may be assured, but its use for the practical purposes of life to the ordinary citizen is more than problematic.

Arabic and Persian are more advantageeously placed in this respect than Sanskrit. Both of them are living languages still spoken by whole populations of men, though, of course, their modern forms are considerably different from the ancient ones. Sanskrit occupies the same position in India that Greek and Latin occupy in Europe. Sensible Europe is dropping the study of these two languages, except for the limited few who aspire to a career of literature, and India will have to drop Sanskrit if she wants her children to employ their time and energy in the solution of the practical problems of life.

The attempt to live in the past is not only futile but even foolish ; what we need to take care of is the future. If India ot the future is to live a full, healthy and vigorous life commensurate with the importance which belongs to it by virtue of its human and other resources, it must come into closer touch with the rest of the world. If it is to occupy its rightful place among the nations of the globe, it must make the most profitable and the most effective use of its intellectual, mental and general human potentialities.

Sanskrit is a perfect language, having a great record of valuable literature, just as Latin and Greek. They are sisters in this respect. But just as Europe and America are discovering that for the ordinary boy not aiming to devote his life to literary or historical research, the study of ancient languages may be profitably displaced by the study of the other modern languages, so will the Hindus ultimately.

That intelligent Hindus already realize this is proved by their conduct. My personal experience (of the last 36 years in connection with the Dayananda Anglo-Vedic College) justifies my saying that of all those who founded the Dayananda Anglo-Vedic College and afterwards nursed it with energy and devotion, there were and are only a few who ever wanted their own children to follow the courses of Sanskrit which they prescribed for others. Of those, perhaps there are still fewer whose sons are using their knowledge of Sanskrit for any effective purpose. Some of them have given up all study of Sanskrit and consider the time spent in acquiring it as lost. Of all those pious donors who make endowments for popularizing the study of Sanskrit or for imparting religious instruction in creeds and forms, there are very few who make their own sons and nephews devote much of their time to either.

Personally, I yield to none in my respect for the ancient Aryans. I am as proud as anyone else of their achievements. They advanced human knowledge to an extent that has made it possible for the moderns to advance further. I am proud of their wisdom, their spirituality, their ethics and their literary achievements, but I cannot shut my eyes to the fact that the world has since then advanced much further in knowledge. And if knowledge is wisdom, then we must presume also that the world is wiser to-day than it was three thousand years ago.

This advanced knowledge and its resultant wisdom is at present embodied in foreign languages. Every year, every month, nay every day, in the year, it is making further progress. So much so that a book dealing with sciences becomes almost out of date within a year, unless a new edition is produced with up-to-date improvements. No one who does not want to fall behind others can afford to neglect these sciences, which can only be studied effectively for at least a number of years in these foreign languages.

Besides it should not be forgotten that modern scientific inventions, including the use of steam and electricity for transportation purposes, have destroyed the barriers of space and distance. No nation, however ideal in its desires and ambitions, however spiritually inclined in its standards and values of life, can live a life of isolation even if it desires to do so. Intercourse with other nations for purposes of trade and commerce is no longer optional. It is compulsory. If India's trade and commerce are to be carried on by Indians and not by foreigners, and if the Indian people are to profit therefrom, it is necessary that our traders and commercial men should know as many modern languages as may be possible for them to acquire first in school and then out of it. The bulk of the nation must be engaged in agriculture, or manufacture, or business. For all these purposes a knowledge of the modern languages is almost a necessity. Under these circumstances to compel boys to devote a greater part of their school time preparatory to entering life in studying a complicated, difficult, ancient language like Sanskrit is such a flagrant misuse of energy that it is bound to harm the general efficiency of the nation if we persist in that course. So it is high time for the nation to make up its mind that the study of Sanskrit, like other luxuries, is for the few and not for the many. Sanskrit must be studied by the few for the purpose of research and culture, and for helping the nation in enriching the vocabulary of the vernaculars. For the many the study of foreign modern languages must be insisted upon, accompanied by a good knowledge of the modern languages of India. I intend to say something more on this subject later. At present I am making these remarks only to clear the ground for the consideration of what would be the aim and scope of any national system of education for India.

Descending from national literature to national methods of education, I must say at once that it will be a folly to revive the latter. They are out of date, and antiquated. To adopt them will be a step backward and not forward.

The present school system is atrocious, and there is no doubt that the ancient system is in certain respects (mark, in certain respects only) much better. The system actually followed at the time of the introduction of British rule had lost the best features of the more ancient one. We are mighty glad that the system then prevalent was rejected in favour of the Western school system. The degeneracy which has resulted from the latter would have been greater and much worse if the former had received the sanction of the State and had been adopted.

The subject is so vast and complicated that it is impossible to discuss it at any length here, but one cannot make himself fully intelligible without making some more observations on the point.

The ancient system which emphasized the personal relationship of the *Guru* and the *Chela* was good in certain respects and harmful in others. The personal relationship supplied the human element which is now missing. This was a guarantee of greater attention being paid to the formation of habits which compose character. On the other hand it had a *tendency* of enslaving the pupil's mind. The aim of education should be to qualify the educated man to think and act for himself with a due sense of responsibility toward society. Did the ancient system achieve this? In my judgment, it could not. The very oath administered to the Brahmchari and the benediction administered by the *Guru*, if properly analysed, will show that the ideal was to reproduce the *Guru* in the person of the *Chela*. The aim of every parent and every teacher should be to enable their children and pupils to be greater and better persons than mere copies of themselves. I shall be glad to be corrected if I am mistaken in this belief. The discipline enforced was too strict, too mechanical, and too empirical. The religion taught was too formal, rigid, and narrow. Disproportionate amount of time was devoted to the memorizing of rules of grammar and texts. It seems that the relations between the teacher and the pupil were possibly freer in the times of the Upanishads than in the period of the Codes. The system inculcated in the Codes is a system of iron and fire.

It was not peculiar to India. The Arabs, the Greeks, and the Latins also had similar systems.

The fact that in spite of this drawback, the Hindu, the Greek, the Roman, the Arab and the Catholic Christian institutions of mediæval Europe produced so many eminent scholars, philosophers and jurists is in no way proof of their excellence. It only establishes the capacity of the human mind to transcend its environments and to rise above the limitations imposed on it by authority, be the authority that of the parent, the *Guru*, or the State.

The Gurukula academy at Hardwar has attempted to remove some of these defects, but I am not quite sure that the segregation insisted on in that institution was ever so complete in the ancient times as it is represented to be. The name implies that the pupil lived with his *Guru* as an adopted member of the latter's family. In every way he was treated as a child of the family. In that case the number that each *Guru* could take must have been extremely limited. There must have been larger *Ashramas* and *Parishads* too where a number of *Gurus* co-operated in teaching and training large numbers of pupils, but whether these *Ashramas* and *Parishads* insisted on the pupils being so completely cut away from society in general is problematic. At any rate the pupils had daily occasions to see and talk to females when they went for *Bhiksha* (food).

I am extremely doubtful if the system of education advocated in the Codes was ever followed universally. I have reason to think that it was mainly devised for the children of the Brahmins. However, be that as it may, I have no doubt that it is impossible to be re-introduced as a part of the general scheme of education in the India of to-day. I am also positive that it is detrimental to the sort of character we want to develop, nay which we must develop, in our boys and girls, if we are to keep pace with the rest of the world, in their march onward. Our boys and girls must not be brought up in hot-houses. They should be brought up in the midst of the society of which they are to be members. They should form habits and learn manners which will enable them to rise to every emergency. They should learn to rise above temptations and not shun them. The world is a temptation. It is a place to enjoy, so long as by doing so one does not injure oneself and others. So long as one is loyal to the society in which his lot has been cast and towards which he has social obligations, one commits no sin by taking to the pleasures of life in a moderate degree.

Boys and girls must learn their social obligations when in their teens. To segregate them at such a time is to deprive them of the greatest and the best opportunity of their lives. The idea of having schools and colleges and universities in localities far away from the bustle of city life and from the temptations incidental to it is an old idea which is being abandoned by the best educational thinkers of the world. The new idea is to let the boys and girls be surrounded by the conditions of life in which they have to move and which they have to meet in later life. To let boys and girls grow in isolation, ignorant of the conditions of actual life, innocent of its social amenities, with no experience of the sudden demands and emergencies of group life, is to deprive them of the most valuable element in their education. The aim of education is to fit men and women for the battle of life; we do not want to convert them into anchorites and ascetics. The boys and girls of to-day are the citizens of to-morrow. From among them must come our statesmen, administrators, generals, inventors, captains of industry and manufacturers, as much as our philosophers and thinkers and teachers. Even sound thinking, to be useful for practical purposes of life, must be based on a full knowledge of the different phases of social life. All life is social. We are beginning to realize that the best social thinkers of the world have been those who were brought up in the full blaze of the social conditions of the time and who had personal experiences of how men in general lived, and how they acted and reacted on each other.

In my judgment, it is not a sound idea to make an anchorite of a boy or a girl. Boys and girls should have every opportunity of seeing life, moving in life, experiencing the shocks and reactions of life and of getting out of the holes into which their animal instincts and their youthful impulses thrust them. Boys brought up in isolation, and girls brought up in *Purdah*, make very poor men and women. Often they have been seen succumbing to the first temptation they came across. They wreck their lives from want of experience and want of nerve. I am speaking from actual experience. Not that men educated in ordinary schools and colleges are always better, but that at least the former have not shown any superiority in handling situations which arise from being thrown into social conditions to which they were strangers before. My experience justifies me in saying that the latter go to greater extremes in laxity of character and looseness of behaviour than the former. They lack the power of adjustment.

It is my desire to impress upon my countrymen, with all the earnestness I possess and with all the emphasis I can lay, the absolute desirability of giving up the antiquated idea of bringing up boys and girls in an atmosphere of isolation. Boys and girls should be treated more as comrades, rather than dependents and inferiors and subordinates. We should extend to them our fullest confidence and encourage absolute frankness in them. Instead of keeping the sexes separate, we should bring them together. In my judgment greater harm is done by keeping them apart than by bringing them together. I know I am treading on delicate ground. Prejudice and sentiment, accumulated by centuries of restricted life, is all against it. The thing will come by degrees. But come it must and come it will.

It will be so much waste of energy not to profit by the experience of other peoples. Our ideas of morality and decency must undergo change. Our boys and girls must grow in an atmosphere of frankness, freedom and mutual confidence. We must do away with suspicion and distrust. It breeds hypocrisy, sycophancy and disease. The future teachers and *Gurus* of India must learn to set aside the tone of command and authority to which they have hitherto been accustomed. The boys and girls are *not* clay in their hands to be moulded into patterns of their choice. That was a stupid idea if ever it existed. They are living beings, products of nature, heredity, and environments. They throb with the same impulses and desires and ideas as we do. These impulses and desires require sane guidance. They cannot be regulated by mere authority, or mainly by authority, without inflicting awful injury on their manhood and womanhood. We command them to do things, of the righteousness and value of which they have not been convinced. The result is a habit of slavish submission to authority. I recognize that we cannot perhaps eliminate the element of command altogether from the education and bringing up of boys and girls. They must, *sometimes*, be protected from themselves. But the command should be the last step, taken with reluctance and out of a sense of unavoidableness which comes by having otherwise failed to arouse an intelligent understanding in the child.

Parents and teachers must learn to respect the child and to have a feeling of reverence for it. No Japanese ever strikes a child, yet the Japanese children are models of reasonableness. The Japanese maintain an attitude of respect towards their children. They treat the children as their equals and always address them as such. They never criticize them harshly. The use of the rod is absolutely unknown in Japanese homes. Harsh language towards children or an expression of anger is very rare. The Japanese code of life is very strict in certain respects. It exacts strict obedience and strict discipline from every citizen. Japanese soldiers have earned a name for their high sense of duty and for strict discipline, but that comes more out of a traditional love for the country and its sovereign, than by enforcing authority and penalties in childhood. In short the system that stresses the authority of the teacher or the parent, which is based on a suspicion of human nature and human tendencies, which is distrustful of childhood, and youth, which is openly out for control and discipline and subordination, which favours empirical methods of pedagogy, which has no respect for the instincts of the boy and the girl, is not an ideal system for the production of self-reliant, aggressive (in order to be progressive) men and women that new India wants. I come to the conclusion, therefore, that any widespread revival of the ancient or mediæval systems of education is unthinkable. It will take us centuries back, and I am certain that the country will not adopt it. Mrs. Besant, of course, does not advocate it. But I know that there are groups of people in India who are in love with that system. They are sometimes carried away by a partial praise of certain features of their system by eminent foreigners and educationalists. A system may be "fascinating," without being sound. It may be highly interesting as an experiment. It may be good for governmental purposes, yet harmful from the citizens' point of view. It may be good for producing certain types, but harmful if adopted for the nation as a whole. I would beg of my countrymen not to be carried off their feet by the praises which the foreigner sometimes bestows on our literature and on our system. Some of them do so out of sheer disgust with their own systems of life. They do not wait to make proper comparisons, but rush from one extreme to another; others only mean to pay a generous compliment. Some perhaps mean mischief. We should not be affected either by their praise or by their condemnation. We are in a critical period of our life, and it behoves us to weigh things in their true perspective, before laying down policies and making plans for constructive upbuilding of the nation. What is required is a sober study of the situation before making plans.

III

THE BROAD AIMS AND IDEALS OF INDIAN EDUCATION

THERE are certain principles and facts which must receive due recognition from those who engage themselves in formulating a scheme of national education for India. I will suggest a few. The first thing to be noted is that education is a vital basic problem. It is not a side issue. It is a fundamental fact of life, individual as well as social. Speaking scientifically, all life is social and so is education, which is the imparting of knowledge by communication. In whichever way you think of education, whether in relation to the individual or to society, the fact, the process, the aim and the substance of education are social. It is a social function. Individuals and society are interdependent ; what is good for the one implies the good of the other.

Education is a means to an end. The end is life and progress, continuous, unending, unhampered. As life admits of no divisions, so progress also is really indivisible into compartments. The division of life into physical, mental, social, ethical and spiritual may be convenient in practice, but is more often than not misleading in principle. Life, a healthy progressive life (that alone is really life), requires a co-operative functioning of all the faculties, with one end. That co-operative end is progress.

Life involves change. Progress is change for the better. Human nature, whatever it may include, is potentially progressive. It is not a fixed, immutable thing, but made pliable indefinitely, though slowly. The law of *Karma* is always working and changing human nature. Individual *Karma* is modified and affected by the social *Karma* and vice versâ.

Social progress is the result of the interplay of various factors which, " albeit they cannot be isolated legitimately from the total organic complex of which each is a part, may for purposes of expansion be distributed under such headings as natural environment, improvement in the arts, social character or development of mental outfit." These may finally be reduced " to one common denominator, mind, in which the elements of desires and rational choice become gradually more distinctive and powerful." That man is a *slave* of his environment is not true.

Growth in freedom is the test of progress. Capacity to rise above one's environment by one's own deliberate effort is freedom. "Growth in freedom is a change in which passive adaptation to nature and instinctive subordination of individual to group becomes active control over nature and emergence of the individual with his voluntary identification of himself and his social group as a possible next step" (Prof. Todd).

There is no happiness without freedom (to the man not free, there is no happiness). Freedom here is not the opposite of physical slavery, but also freedom as far as possible from the *bondage* of desires and environments. Growth of freedom in an individual means growth of mastery over self, in every way, though it does not involve his being desocialized. What is true of individuals, in this respect, is also true of an individual social group or a nation. It is not the size of a nation that is the chief determinant in its progress. "Not big populations but *sound, efficient, integrated populations* are potentially progressive." Integration does not mean uniformity or "dead levelism."

It signifies oneness in purpose and oneness in spirit—a spirit of co-operation and co-ordination in all the phases of national life and national activity.

The first aim of all sound education then should be to teach the individual that the growth towards freedom is progress; that every human being is the master of his own destiny; that neither fate nor *Karma* is above control; that the road to progress lies in the voluntary identification of oneself with his or her social group; that the nation is that social group with which every person should identify himself or herself; that without this identification progress or growth towards freedom is indeed very difficult, if not altogether impossible.

The tendency of popular beliefs and customs and characteristics in India is toward an undue insistence on the driving force of *Kismet* and *Karma*. Our people require to be assiduously and persistently taught that there is no such thing as *Kismet*, and that *Karma* is always controllable and manageable by one's own efforts as well as by changes in one's social environments. Hinduism does not teach a belief in *Kismet*, but its insistence on the driving force of *Karma* is somewhat enervating and emasculating. Greater emphasis should be laid on one's ability to change, over-ride or counteract,—in a word, to control his *Karma*—by thought and action in this life, made possible and supported by social environments.

Mohammedanism, too, does not inculcate a belief in *Kismet*; yet it cannot be denied that the current tendency even there is to rely too much on *Kismet*.

It is also necessary that the importance of social environments be actively promulgated.

The old idea that geography and blood control the social characteristics of a people is being demonstrably disproved, and no pains should be spared to free the Indian mind from this superstition which is finding so much reinforcement by the writings of sophisticated philosophers and historians of the West. Climatic conditions do play an important part in the formation of national characteristics, but their influence, wherever evil or harmful to progress, can be counteracted and modified by active efforts. Similarly, too much importance is being given to race, blood, and heredity. We are being continually told that not only our geographical surroundings, but our blood inheritance incapacitates us from political progress on democratic lines.

"Inherent differences in 'racial vitality,'" remarks Professor Todd, "though frequently asserted, are by no means demonstrated." Brain weight, he adds, "corresponds in no way to degree of intelligence. Craniometry is of no value in attempting to fix racial differences. Recent studies in human pigmentation show that it, too, is not a fundamental mark of social character. Skin pigment is a protection against too much sunlight and varies with intensity of sunlight."

The Indian mind has for some centuries been more or less in a state of captivity. The strict regulated life of the *Shastras* and the *Shara*, the rule of the priest, the lack of opportunities for education, the constantly disturbed conditions of the country, the philosophical pessimism of the creeds and the cults, the belittling of life by centuries of monasticism and asceticism, all had for some time combined to make life in India static rather than dynamic. Voices were from time to time raised against the gross forms of worship and ritual followed by the people, but they were not powerful enough to make an effective crusade against ignorance. The result is that the India of the last thousand years has been more decadent than progressive—often going backward, rather than forward.

The problem before us, so far as it touches our past, is two-fold. Our critics and calumniators assure us that we have been and are a "barbarous" people, that "there never was a civilization in India," that our case is that of "arrested progress," and that we have never achieved anything remarkable in the world of thought, or discovery, or invention, or action. In short, that we have been more or less parasites. A radical critic has, in a recent book, denounced what he calls our national self-complacency, in no measured terms. In the early days of British rule, James Mill (the English radical) and the Christian fathers did the same. Then with the "discovery" of Sanskrit and the literature contained therein, with the translation of parts of that literature into the European languages (though even often crude and incorrect), and with the bit by bit construction of ancient Indian history, there came a change. The European world began to appreciate the achievements of the ancient Indians in the domain of thought and knowledge quite enthusiastically, and the Indians themselves rose one morning to find that the best minds of the world recognized in them the descendants of men who were their equals in brain power of every kind. This raised them considerably in self-estimation, and they began to use the greatness of their past as a lever and as an inspiration for aspirations of greatness in the future. In this they achieved a notable success. The renaissance in India is its outcome.

In this process, however, *some* of us lost the sense of proportion. In our anxiety to reply to our critics tit for tat, we began to make extravagant claims for our ancestors, and to trace to India all that is good, true, and beautiful in the world. Even this, perhaps, would not have mattered, had we not started making extravagantly disparaging statements about modern civilization, thus claiming for ourselves a sort of monopoly in truth and wisdom and art. Mr. William Archer's book, "India and the Future," is the retort. Now this question of the proper valuation of our civilization and of our standards of life has been complicated by the bearing it has on politics. We suspect, quite naturally and not without justification, that the object of our traducers is to affect our national psychology so detrimentally as to stop us from making claims of equality with the ruling race. The point has been so well explained by Professor Ross of Wisconsin (U.S.A.), in a book on Russia (" Russia in Upheaval," The Century Company, New York, 1918), that I cannot do better than quote his words. They have the additional merit of being directed against Germany. Speaking of certain excellent traits in Russian character either not noticed at all or belittled by their German traducers, Professor Ross remarks :—

> It is a discernment of these precious traits in the Russian nature that causes all Americans who know them well to prophesy a great future for the Russians after they have come into their own. We recognize that in some ways their instincts are better adapted to a co-operative and democratic social order than are ours. But just at this point appears a significant divergence of opinion between Americans and German observers of Russia. All the educated Germans I sounded, from Courland landlords to Lutheran pastors along the Volga, harped on the low state of culture among the Russian masses and their anarchic tendency, called for a firm hand to hold them in, and predicted that an immense time would elapse before they could attain the strength of character, steadiness of purpose, and capacity for self-determination of West Europeans. Generally, " two or three centuries " of tutelage was deemed necessary. On the contrary,

Americans with equally full knowledge of the people attribute their backwardness to specific and recently operative causes, such as isolation, autocracy, serfdom, ignorance, and the communal system. They anticipate that under good conditions, the mentality of the masses may be speedily improved, and they never put off the date of "arrival" of the Russians later than the end of this century.

Now, the latter opinion tallies closely with that of science. No doubt nineteen out of twenty French or American sociologists—the acknowledged leaders in this branch—would agree that if Russians are vouchsafed a peaceful, democratic development and speedily employ on a great scale such agencies as private property in land, free institutions, schools, and libraries, their great-grandchildren may attain any level of culture now in the world. Why, then, do the Germans alone insist that it will take the Russians centuries to "catch up"? Simply because it has been the policy of the ruling element in Germany to encourage the type of social philosophy that makes a backward people distrusted by itself and by the world.

Russia has been Germany's farm. She has been against the emancipation of the masses there, because she wishes to preserve in Russia the widest possible field for German merchants, technicians, opticians, pharmacists, managers, and engineers; also she desires a field for German wares and the investment of German capital. Anything she can do to discourage Russians and to deter them from adopting the institutions that quickly raise a backward people prolongs her farming of them. In a word, the Kultur theory put forth by Germany's professors and publicists in the name of science is but a special poison gas!

A people constantly belittled by the foreigner, as well as by their own leaders, gets no chance of cultivating the necessary qualities of self-respect and self-confidence. People wanting in these qualities are on the surest road to decay and annihilation. Hence the necessity, the absolute necessity, of counteracting the evil effects of such sweeping denunciations of all our institutions. Our critics call us essentially backward; in season and out of season, they harp on the diversity of race, religion and language in India, and insist that we are unfit for progress on democratic lines or that the progress that we can make must *necessarily* be slow, very slow, so slow indeed that they cannot see the possibility of responsible government in India in any distance of time which they can foresee. Yet it is these mentors of ours who have so far refused even elementary instruction in the three R's to our masses, and have persistently declined to make adequate provision for vocational education for our children. It is they who are interested in keeping us caste-ridden and tied down to the superstitions of despotic rule. It is our bounden duty to counteract the evil effects of these insinuations by pointing out to our people the glories of our past and the merits of our institutions. But the process of self-praise and the glorification of our past has its dangerous side also. It has the tendency of making us look to the past, rather than to the future, thus sometimes blinding us to the progress which the world has made since ancient Aryan times.

If modern truths (truth is truth and is neither ancient nor modern) are to be tested by the sanctions of the ancient times, and to be promulgated only if they accord with the teachings of our *Rishis*, then woe to India. It is quite another thing to find evidences of the modern improvements in the ancient books and use the authority of the latter as an additional argument for their promulgation and acceptance. But to reject them because of their being opposed to, or inconsistent with, the dicta of the ancient *Rishis* is blocking the road to progress. No progress is conceivable unless we have an open mind and do away with the superstition that all truth was revealed to us in the beginning of the world and that all that was worth knowing was known to our ancestors, and that they had said the last word on all questions, be they religion, or sociology, or politics, or economics, or art, or even science. It is essential that we should realize that we are living in a new world, a world quite different from the one in which our ancestors lived, in many respects much more advanced than the latter, in some respects possibly not so advanced. Our progress will depend on our capacity to strike the golden mean and to preserve a well-balanced attitude towards the past and the present, with the determination to chalk out a future for ourselves greater than our past. Under the present circumstances there is little danger of our enemies succeeding in persuading us to believe that we are an inferior race, or that we have nothing to be proud of in our past, or that we lack the necessary quality of adjusting ourselves to the needs and requirements of the present. On the other hand there is some danger of our being self-complacent by overestimating the merits of our own civilization to the disparagement of the modern. We cannot be too much on guard against this danger. Subject to these observations I am in full agreement with Mrs. Besant that "national education must live in an atmosphere of proud and glowing patriotism," and that "this atmosphere must be kept sweet, fresh and bracing by the study of Indian literature, Indian history, etc." It is most important then to consider how to achieve that end without its harmful tendencies.

IV

THE PROBLEM

As I have already remarked above, our problem is two-fold. We have to remove the causes and destroy the influences that created the atmosphere of despondency and pessimism into which the country was sunk immediately before the birth of the new nationalist movement. For that purpose we have to construct the history of our past, and to establish by documentary evidence of the best kind that there is nothing in our heredity which inherently unfits us for the great rôle to which we are aspiring. On the evidence already published, we can very well defend our past against the calumnies that are often circulated to prove our inherent or ingrained incapacity for great achievements, whether in the domain of thought or action. It is not necessary for us for that purpose to claim that our civilization was in every respect superior to the modern civilization, nor that our ancestors enjoyed the monopoly of spiritual insight or of divine wisdom. It is sufficient that at no period of our history, except within the last 200 years, were we in a position of inferiority, either culturally or otherwise, to the other nations of the world as they were then. The civilization we developed was noble, lofty and great. Our achievements in religion, philosophy, law, sociology, sciences and arts are worthy of being compared with the best of the old world. They do not sink into insignificance even when compared with the best of the modern world. We have no reason to be ashamed of our past. On the contrary, we have every reason to be proud of it. But that does not mean that our ancestors have spoken the last word on every conceivable subject.

Humanity is progressing. Human knowledge is advancing. Man's power over nature is increasing. Civilization owes us a deep debt of gratitude for having provided it with sound foundations and solid scaffolding and for having erected the lower stories of the edifice. Our people are inferior to none, either in mental or physical capacities. Given opportunities and favourable circumstances, we can hold our own in competition with any other people of the earth. By co-operation we can make substantial contributions to the progress of humanity. We cannot afford to neglect a single opportunity of impressing all this on our own people as well as on the foreigners who do not know us well.

Under no circumstances must we allow our people to think of themselves in terms of self-depreciation, nor can we allow the foreigners to condemn us on racial grounds or assume our cultural inferiority. We must keep our heads erect, and must continue to cultivate self-respect and self-confidence in ourselves and to instil them in our boys and girls. A man who begins to think himself low is on the right road to become low. Our mentors in the Imperial Press have been playing that game persistently. In that sense I heartily endorse Mrs. Besant's exhortation to do away with all apologies and explanations on behalf of India, her religions, her customs and her institutions. We owe no apologies and explanations to anyone. Bona-fide friendly criticism we welcome. We are glad to profit therefrom. But general denunciation, based on racial arrogance, racial bias or prejudice we resent. On this point we cannot be too sensitive.

Yet, as also already observed, we have to be very careful against self-complacency, self-conceit, and an assumption of perfection in our institutions and ideas. Not to be alive to our weaknesses, to the correction of our social standards, to the degeneration of our religious values and to the reactionary and even barbaric nature of some of our customs will be a fatal hindrance to progress. We must go to the root causes of the same to apply fundamental cures. In our march onward, we shall have to destroy a good deal before we can put up new structures necessary for our progress and worthy of our position in the family of nations. We cannot assume that everything ancient was perfect and ideal. Some of the ideas held by our ancestors have been proved to be wrong; we have to readjust them. Some of their methods were faulty; we have to improve upon them. Some of their institutions, very well suited to their age and conditions, are absolutely unsuited to modern conditions of life; we must replace them. We do not want to be a mere copy of our ancestors. We wish to be better.

With that object we have to re-value our standards and ideals. The task requires all our courage and manliness. It needs unity, co-operation, and concerted action. Above all it needs self-confidence and self-realization, individual as well as national. We shall welcome all aid, but *we will depend on ourselves only*. It is in this spirit that we should approach the problem of national education. Assume nothing, analyse every idea, examine every scheme in the light of the day, in the searchlight of scientific truth. Let our schemes be tested by the most critical tests of the times. Let us compare them with what people are thinking, saying and doing in other countries. After all these processes have been gone through, let us take counsel with one another and decide on our future course. We do not want to be English or German or American or Japanese ; true, we want to be Indians, but modern, up-to-date, progressive Indians, proud of our past and aspiring to a greater and a nobler future.

What do we mean by national education ? Do we want to distinguish it from local and provincial education, or from denominational or sectarian education ? How does education become national ? Is it the language which is the medium of instruction, which makes it national, or the agency through which it is imparted, or the agency which controls and regulates it, or the books which are taught or the standards and ideals which underlie it?

Truth is neither local nor national nor even international. It is simply truth. Science and philosophy expound truth. Are we going to reject the sciences and the philosophy of the western scientists and philosophers, because the discoverers of these sciences and the writers of books on philosophy happened to be non-Indians? Are we going to reject Shakespeare, Bacon, Goethe, Schiller, Emerson, Whitman, because they were not Indians? How shall we feel if the Europeans reject everything Indian? Are we going to discontinue learning the modern sciences of medicine, surgery, pathology, hygiene, engineering (civil, mechanical, electrical, agricultural, and mining), botany, geology, zoology, etc., because they are so much advanced from the things that we have in our literature on these subjects? Then what about the modern sciences of navigation, commerce, banking, insurance, etc.? Are we going back to the old methods? Shall we reject the modern improvements?

Last, but not least, what about politics and civics and sociology? What is our "national" political system? Let me say once for all, that except for historical purposes, it is sheer and unjustifiable waste of time to insist on the dissemination of theories that have been superseded by and discarded in favour of others proved to be better and truer than the former. For example, it will be sheer folly to replace the modern treatises on arithmetic, geometry, algebra, trigonometry and kindred subjects, by *Liláwati* or other books on these subjects, found in the Sanskrit language. Our *Arthashastra* may have been excellent in the good old times. It may do us good to study it for the purposes of comparison. If there is anything in it which is still valuable we may adopt it, but we will be cutting our nose to spite our faces if we fail to insist on the teaching of the modern and the up-to-date *Arthashastra*, which controls and orders the economic life of the world.

We have of late heard a great deal about the desirability of reviving the *Ayurvedic* and the *Unání* systems of medicine. I have a certain amount of sympathy with the movement. But if there are any people in India who would do away with the modern medical college and replace modern medicine and surgery by the old "Jarráhí," then all I can say is, God help India. We lose millions of valuable lives, particularly of women and children, because we are ignorant of the modern methods of midwifery and child-nursing. We require a widespread dissemination of these. We cannot go back to the traditional methods of bringing our men and women into the world and then letting them die by hundreds in every thousand in order to be more truly national.

As to the *Dharmashastra* again, I must say that however desirable it may be for us to be acquainted with our own laws and social sciences, the current treatises are full of crude, absurd, inconsistent, diametrically antagonistic views and theories. We cannot afford to tax the mental capacity of our children by placing in their hands the current editions of *Manu*, *Nárada*, and *Apasthamba*, without subjecting them to major operations. They *must* form a part of the courses of higher study. They must be digested and studied very carefully, because otherwise we shall not be able to found the new social philosophy we need so much. But that does not mean that we can ignore with impunity a study of the statute-made laws of modern India, or a study of the laws of other countries. A study of the modern laws, of civics, of the modern world, of the forms of government prevailing in other countries, of their politics and economics, is a *sine qua non* of future progress on healthy lines. These things ought to be taught to every boy and girl, even in elementary schools. It is only their widespread dissemination that will make us politically self-conscious and alert. It will strengthen us in our political aspirations, warn us against pitfalls, vivify our finances and guide us in our economic readjustments. Then what about the modern science of arms and the art of war? Are we going to re-introduce the bow and arrow or the matchlock gun, or fighting with swords and spears? If so, then woe to us.

I have said all this, not because Mrs. Besant meant anything of the kind, but because there are some good people in India, who do, now and then, talk of the desirability of their country leading a retired, isolated and self-contained life. They pine for good old days and wish them to come back. They sell books, which contain this kind of nonsense. They write poems and songs, full of soft sentimentality.[1] I do not know

[1] In order to guard against being misunderstood, let me say that this does not apply to the works of Rabindranath Tagore.

whether they are idiots or traitors. I must warn my countrymen most solemnly and earnestly to beware of them and of that kind of literature. We must realize once for all that no country on the face of the globe can, under modern conditions, live an isolated and self-contained life, even if she desires to do so. The world would not let us alone, even if we wished to be let alone. A country occupying a space of about two million square miles, with a population of one-fifth of the human race, cannot and will not be let alone. If the sons of the soil fail to develop it and its resources, others will. The country must be brought up to the level of the most modern countries not only in politics and economics, but even in thought and life, if we want to keep it for ourselves and our children and save it from the foreign exploiter. It is true we do not want India to become England or France or Japan or America. We want it to remain India. We would not be Indians, if we did not want to remain Indians. But let us understand once for all, that under modern conditions of life, the distinction between this country and the others is destined to be much less than it used to be before the introduction of steam and electricity in human affairs. Climatic, environmental, racial, linguistic, social, traditional and historical distinctions will not be effaced, but they will be considerably reduced both in volume and in kind. The world is tending to become one family. Anyone who aspires or plans to obstruct the process is a traitor to his country as well as to humanity at large. Strong, brainy, powerful, resourceful people have nothing to fear from the process ; weak, backward, effeminate, soft, unadaptable people will either be exterminated in the end or will continue to be exploited by others.

Fundamental human nature is the same all the world over. The differences are mostly social, linguistic, climatic. It is extremely doubtful if racial differences are so radical and well marked as they are sometimes represented to be. Linguistic and climatic differences will remain, but social and political and economic differences will disappear or at any rate will be effectively lessened. Let people come to the United States of America and study the problem in this great melting-pot of humanity. This great war has proved the intensity of existing national differences, but in my judgment it has also established the oneness of humanity and the probability, in the not very remote future, of world unity and a world culture. The whole world seems to be in the melting-pot. Those who doubt it should travel over the world and see how difficult it is to distinguish men of one nationality from another in the streets of New York, Paris, London, Berlin, and Tokio. New York, Chicago, Washington (D.C.), and San Francisco are miniature worlds in themselves. You find all races and nations and languages and cultures represented there. Fair-coloured people of all nationalities, living in the same way, speaking the same language, appear to be all alike. Walking in the streets of New York, sometimes it seems that every third man speaks a language other than English, but not knowing all the languages of the world, that fact alone gives you no clue to the nationality of the speaker. One talks of the shape of the nose, of the head, of the colour of the hair, etc., but reliance on any of these so-called distinctive marks is oftener than not misleading. Dip into the East-end avenues of New York, and you will be unable to distinguish between an Armenian, a Persian, a Syrian, a fair-coloured Arab, a Russian, a Turk, a Red

Indian, a fair-coloured Hindu, an Egyptian, a German, an Italian, a Pole, a Swiss, a Swede, a Norwegian, a Finn, a Hungarian, a Bulgarian, a Dane, a Spaniard or a Portuguese, even a light-coloured Negro. You can often point out a Chinese or a Japanese, but sometimes you make mistakes even about them. I have seen many Chinese and Japanese dressed in European clothes, in the United States and in Japan, whom it was impossible to distinguish from Europeans. One can have no idea of how fast Japan is being Europeanized. One may deplore it, one may rebuke the Japanese for adopting European manners, but the fact remains that the Japanese could not and cannot help it. The process is almost universal.

It is true a uniform world will be hideous. It is more beautiful and sublime in its variety. But whether we wish it or not, that variety is going to disappear, at least superficially. No, perhaps I am not right. It will not disappear altogether, but it will be reduced very very appreciably in the course of the next two centuries. Even in thought and life it is going to be materially altered and affected. In my judgment, the best interests of humanity lie in reducing the differences and bringing into prominence the points of contact and the similarities. The culture of the Anglo-Saxon, the *Kultur* of the Teutons, the civilization of the Latins are all going to shake hands. Their essence will be the same. The ambitions of their professors and savants may clash and conflict, but their general life will be the same.

The same may be said of Asia. The time is near when the Arabs, the Persians, the Hindus, the Chinese and the Japanese will more readily talk of the things common to them, than of their differences. It may seem strange, it may look humiliating, but the unity of Asia is going to be brought about by Europe and European thought. Fear of Europe will unite Asia, and then the fear of Asia in its turn will bring about the unity of Europe and Asia. With Europe and Asia united, the world becomes one. America is a child of Europe, and native Africa is more or less a child of Asia. Both of them, in their own ways, are going to help the process of assimilation, integration, and unity. Out of this world war (or it may be wars) will emerge world unity.

In my judgment it will be folly and madness to try to discourage the study and dissemination of European languages, European literatures and European sciences in

India. The fact is that we have not had enough of them. Circumstances have so far kept us away from them. We should strain every nerve to spread and disseminate them until every Indian knows at least one European language, has European tools in his hands, and easily handles European mechanical appliances. Europe and the world have learnt a great deal from us; we have no reason to be ashamed of learning from them, with the fullest intention of adding to their knowledge and teaching them in our turn.

V

THE RIGHT HONOURABLE MR. FISHER ON EDUCATIONAL PROBLEMS OF ENGLAND

The capital of a country does not consist in cash or paper, but in the brains and bodies of the people who inhabit it . . .—THE RIGHT HONOURABLE MR. FISHER, President of the Board of Education.

RIGHT in the middle of the war, the greatest war of the world, at the time of the greatest danger to the country and the Empire, Mr. Fisher, the minister responsible for the control of education in England, has been considering and enforcing consideration by the nation and the Parliament of the question of national education. In the Preface to a pamphlet called "Educational Reform," which is a collection of his speeches on the subject, delivered in 1917 in and outside Parliament, he observes :—

Obviously education is important. Everybody who has a child knows that the future of his child depends upon the way he is brought up. Is he to be competent for the business of life or incompetent, *a profitable member of the community or a parasite*? Is he to be prudent or profligate, cultured or ignorant, brutal or refined, social or anti-social, *a citizen or an anarchist*? The answer to all these questions is to be found partly in descent; but far more largely in circumstances which, unlike the unalterable traits handed down in blood, can be affected for better or for worse by education.[1]

After these basic remarks, Mr. Fisher proceeds to consider if there is any force in the adverse criticism of popular education, made by classes interested to keep the masses down. These latter have often been heard speaking of popular education with contempt. "They are prepared to believe that it is good for well-to-do people—for the aristocracy of the human race," but not for the common people, whose task it is to toil with their hands and produce the things of the world for the use of the former, their natural leaders. They admit that "Education should be somewhere, but deny that it should be everywhere." "I wish to prove," adds Mr. Fisher, "that it should be everywhere, and that no state can flourish without a sound popular system of education."

[1] The italics in this quotation are mine.—L. R.

We have to "conceive of education as drawing out of a man all that is best and most useful in him so that it may be employed to the advantage of the community and of himself as a member of it. We must regard it not as bearing fruit in the science and art of earning a livelihood *alone*, but as yielding *the science and art of living*. It is the means by which the individual citizen may be trained to make the best use of his innate qualities and the means by which the State may be enabled to make the best use of its citizens. Spiritually conceived it is Plato's 'turning of the soul towards the light'; materially conceived it is Napoleon's 'open career to talent.' In any case it is of great democratic interest, for indeed a wise democratic Government is impossible without it."

The remarks which follow next show that it is not in India alone that people are dissatisfied with the education imparted in public schools, but that the complaint is directed against the public schools of the British Isles as well.

I have heard people say (observes Mr. Fisher) that much of our present education is very poor stuff, and that if we drop into a school and listen to the lessons we are apt to find *that the wrong things are being taught by the wrong people in the wrong way.* But if this be so, who is responsible? The culprit is the nation. . . . It cannot be too urgently represented that the future of the children of the people, so far as it is affected by education, depends upon the number of men and women in the community who can be found to insist upon a high educational standard in their several localities. . . .

Until the people of this country [i.e. Great Britain] come to view education as the most fruitful of all benefits which age can confer upon youth, and not as one of those troublesome ailments of childhood which must be got through as quickly as possible, it is vain to expect any great improvement in the standard of our National Schools.

Mr. Fisher, analysing this criticism of popular education a little in detail, says:

Education is apt to evoke in many minds the idea of a little dull book-learning drilled into a reluctant brain by a deadening machine. Such, indeed, it once was, and so in some backward parts of the country (alas! too many) it may still be; but if we take our present elementary school at its best, and consider the general conception of educational policy which animates our present practice, the description would be grotesquely unfair. We have made great strides towards a better method and a wider and more catholic view. Books, of course, remain, as they always should, the principal fashioning instrument of the mind; but they no longer stand alone. The training of hand, eye, ear, and voice supplement the older and central discipline of literature, opening new windows into the world and quickening the senses to new forms of happy exercise.

Having thus defended the present public school education in England, Mr. Fisher then descends to the very palpable nature of the deficiencies which remain to be cured, and which, in the French phrase, "leap to the eyes." Some of these are stated in the following sentence :—

"It has also been long evident not only *that the State contribution was insufficient in amount* and that an undue share of *the schools were undermanned* and the *teachers underpaid.*" The duty of the State in this respect is stated thus :—

But though the State cannot forbid wage-earning among young people [why it cannot, we don't see (L. R.)], it should and must assign a value to learning as well as to earning. *It has a right and a duty to affirm that it believes in education for the masses,* and that by education it means not a sham and make-believe, but something substantial, something which will leave a durable mark on mind and character, and that the claim of this education on the child is paramount. Then if it be found that the minimum upon which the State insists cannot in all cases be secured without inflicting real hardship, those cases of hardship should be separately met. The State should not allow itself to be diverted from its great object of diffusing knowledge and intelligence among the people, by the fear of being involved in some expenditure based on personal circumstances. It should first devise a course of education, as thorough and effective as the object demands and the available means of instruction furnish, and then, having settled on a plan likely to *give to each of its citizens the fullest chance for self-development*, it should be prepared to give adequate assistance in special cases.

Mr. Fisher then confidently pronounces that the present amount of education obtained by the great majority of the population is " inadequate " to the " present and future needs " of the British nation, and says that :—

If we ask whether, as a result of all this training in our schools, the great mass of our population is getting out of life as much value as life can give them, having regard to their material circumstances, there can be only one answer, and that answer is that millions of our countrymen and countrywomen are making very little use of their lives for want of an agency which may direct and educate them and their sense of value during the whole period of youth.

In a word, he adds, "our system is half-hearted."

" Meanwhile the conditions of modern industrial life are steadily increasing the dangers of under-education. Processes are becoming more mechanical and monotonous, as they become standardized and subdivided, with the natural result that a claim is made for shorter hours and larger leisure," and, I may add, for better skilled knowledge in the use of these processes. The whole argument is then summed up in the following pithy paragraph :—

> . . . *The province of popular education is to equip the men and women of this country for the tasks of citizenship.* All are called upon to live, many are called upon to die, for the community of which they form a part. That they should be rescued from the dumb helplessness of ignorance is, if not a precept of the eternal conscience, at least an elementary part of political prudence, to which the prospective enfranchisement of several million new voters . . . adds a singular emphasis. But the argument does not rest upon grounds of political prudence alone, but upon *the right of human beings to be considered as ends in themselves,* and to be entitled, so far as our imperfect social arrangements may permit, to know and enjoy all the best that life can offer in the sphere of knowledge, emotion and hope.

In his first speech in the House of Commons on April 19th, 1917, introducing the Education estimates, Mr. Fisher expressed his gratification at the "quickened perception of the true place of education in the scheme of public welfare" brought about by the war, resulting "in a very earnest resolve to give to our national system all the improvements of which it is capable."

In making a plea for an additional grant for education, after citing the figures relating to the expenditure on education in England —" Some £16,000,000 are paid out of the taxes, another £17,000,000 out of the rates, and perhaps, though it is impossible to make an exact calculation, a sum of £7,000,000 out of fees, voluntary contributions and endowments" (this makes a total of £40,000,000, or 60 crores of rupees in Indian coin)—Mr. Fisher says: " But when we are considering a form of productive expenditure which is not only *an investment but an insurance*, that question cannot stand alone. We must ask a supplementary question. We must ask not only whether *we can afford to spend the money*." He calls the supplementary question " more important and more searching." He then goes into the defects of the existing system and machinery of education in England, and finally sums up as below :—

What is it that we desire, in a broad way, for our people ? That they should be good citizens, reverent and dutiful, sound in mind and body, skilled in the practice of their several avocations, and capable of turning their leisure to a rational use. And what do we see? Our level of physique as a nation is deplorably below the standard which a great people should set before itself. Our common taste in amusement is still in the main rude and uncultured. We have lost and are only now slowly beginning to recapture something of that general taste in music which was long ago a special note of our English civilization. . . . Our aptitude for technological studies is great, but only half-developed . . . We are only just beginning to realize that the capital of a country does not consist in cash or paper, but in the brains and bodies of the people who inhabit it.

He ends with a plea for a change on the additional ground of the universal cry for economy, " we should *economize in the human capital of the country, our most precious possession, which we have too long suffered to run to waste.*"

In his second speech, delivered in the same place, while introducing a new Education Bill, on August 10, 1917, Mr. Fisher describes some aspects of the movements of opinion which, in the minds of the Government, have made a considerable measure of advance in education an absolute necessity. " In the first place, attention has been increasingly directed to the close connection between educational and physical efficiency. One of the great dates in our social history is the establishment of the school medical service in 1907. We now know what we should not otherwise have known, how greatly the value of our educational system is impaired by the low physical conditions of a vast number of the children, and how imperative is the necessity of raising the general standard of physical health among the children of the poor, if the great part of the money spent on our educational system is not to be wasted. Another element is the growing consciousness that there is a lack of scientific co-relation between the different parts of our educational machinery. . . . . . Everyone realizes the elementary fact that some children, if they are only given opportunity, will profit most through modern language and history, others by a scientific and technical education, and others again are destined by their turn of mind to profit most from an education based largely on the study of classical antiquity. But under our existing system we have no security that in any 'area of accessibility,' to adopt a vague but convenient term, these various needs and aptitudes will be provided for. There is not even a reasonable probability that the child will get the higher education best adapted to his or her needs. . ."

A third feature in the movement of opinion is the increased feeling of social solidarity which has been created by the war, " which leads people to realize that the boundaries of citizenship are not determined by wealth, and that the same logic which leads us to desire an extension of the franchise points also to an extension of education."

Upon this basis Mr. Fisher explains the different provisions of the Bill under six heads :—

First, we desire to improve the administrative organization of education.

Secondly, we are anxious to secure for every boy and girl in this country an elementary school life up to the age of fourteen, which shall be unimpeded by the competing claims of industry.

Thirdly, we desire to establish part-time day continuation schools which every young person in the country shall be *compelled* to attend unless he or she is undergoing some suitable form of alternative instruction.

Fourthly, we make a series of proposals for the development of the higher forms of elementary education and for the improvement of the physical condition of the children and young persons under instruction.

Fifthly, we desire to consolidate the elementary school Grants, and

Sixthly, we wish to make an effective survey of the whole educational provision in the country, and to bring private educational institutions into closer and more convenient relations to the national system.

I do not propose to reproduce his detailed statements and arrangements under each of these heads, but I must give the following extract illustrating what he means by " comprehensive schemes ":—

First, we want to make it plain that the education given in our public elementary schools is not to be considered an end in itself, but as a stage in the child's education destined to lead to a further stage. Secondly, we propose to require local educational authorities under Part III of the Education Act of 1902 to make adequate provision, either by special classes or by means of central schools, for what may be termed higher elementary education. We desire to meet the objection which is commonly, and not without justice, advanced against so much of the work done in our public elementary schools during the last two years—that the children are marking time, that their education is not bringing them on, and that it does not fit them for their future calling. We desire to change all that, and our Bill provides not only for the introduction of practical instruction at appropriate stages, but for the preparation of children for further education in schools other than elementary, and for their transference at suitable ages to such schools.

I pass now to a series of proposals which are designed to improve and to strengthen our existing fabric of elementary education so as to secure for every child in the kingdom a sound physique and a sound groundwork of knowledge before the period when the part-time system begins. We propose to encourage the establishment of nursery schools for children under five years, and to empower the local education authorities to raise the age at which normal instruction in the elementary schools begins to six, as soon as there is an adequate supply of nursery schools for the younger children in the area. We propose to amend the law of school attendance so as to abolish all exemptions between the ages of five and fourteen, and we propose to place further restrictions upon the employment of children during the elementary school period.

He ends his speech by a general summary of the objects of the Bill :—

We assume that education is one of the good things of life which should be more widely shared than has hereto been the case among the children and young persons of the country. We assume that *education should be the education of the whole man, spiritually, intellec'ua'ly, and physically, and that it is not beyond the resources of civilization to devise a scheme of education, possessing certain common qualities, but admitting at the same time of large variation from which the whole youth of the country, male and female, may derive benefit.* We assume that the principles upon which well-to-do parents proceed in the education of their families are valid also *mutatis mutandis* for the families of the poor; that the State has need to secure for its juvenile population conditions under which mind, body, and character may be harmoniously developed.

We feel also that in the existing circumstances the life of the rising generation can only be protected against the injurious effects of industrial pressure by a further measure of State compulsion. But we argue that the compulsion proposed in this Bill will be no sterilizing restriction of wholesome liberty, but an essential condition of a larger and more enlightened freedom, which will tend to stimulate civic spirit, to promote general culture and technical knowledge, and to diffuse a steadier judgment and a better informed opinion through the whole body of the community.

The pamphlet "Educational Reform" includes five more speeches delivered by Mr. Fisher at Manchester, Liverpool, Bradford, before the Lancashire Teachers' Association in 1917, and before the Training College Association in January, 1918. The principles enunciated in these speeches are the same which I have quoted from the speeches made by him in the House of Commons, but there are some very apt phrases which are calculated to emphasize certain phases of the problem, which might well be collected in one place for facility of future reference.

In the speech delivered at Manchester on September 25, 1917, he characterized the Education Bill as a measure "for the diminution of ignorance, unhappiness, misconduct and disease."

I venture to plead for a state of society in which learning comes first and earning comes second among the obligations of youth, not for one class only, but for all young people. At present the rich learn and the poor earn.

Education is the eternal debt which maturity owes to youth. Now I do not care whether youth be poor or rich, we owe it education—all the education which it can afford to receive and all the education which we can afford to give.

At Bradford he said :—

My point of view is that education is one of the most precious goods of life, and that the more fully and equally it can be distributed the more happy we shall be, and the stronger will be our community. And this belief in the value of education has been very much deepened by the experience of this country during the war. Have you ever reflected, ladies and gentlemen, upon the astonishing influence which education has exercised over the course of this titanic conflict ; how those countries have best succeeded who have equipped themselves with a modern provision of education, and how those countries have succeeded least who have been most backward in their provision of popular education ? I suppose there has never been a war in which the contending armies have been so well educated, or in which the contending armies have owed so much to science and education. And whether you talk to the officers at the front—who will all speak to you of the value which they attach to a well-educated non-commissioned officer or private—or whether you go to the headquarters' staff, or whether you go to the great munition factories and sources of military supply, you always have the same answer to the same question. Always you will be told that education is the keynote of efficiency.

When I began my survey of national education I was struck—as I suppose everybody is struck—by the fact that there are millions and millions of men and women in this country who are not getting as much out of life as life can afford to give them. There are millions of men and women who derive no profit from books, no pleasure from music or pictures, very little cultivated joy from the ordinary beauties of nature. They pass their life bound down to dull mechanical toil, harnessed to iron and steel, without a gleam of poetry, without a touch of imagination, with the faintest sense of the glories and splendours of the world in which we live, unable to attach to their ordinary dull task the interest which belongs to a scientific appreciation of the principles upon which that task is founded, unable equally to turn their leisure to any rational or cultivated account; and I ask myself this: Ought we to be content with a state of civilization in which these things are possible, and should it not be part of our duty so to provide for posterity that they may have within their reach a happier, more cultivated, and wider life?

In conclusion:—

This is a people's measure. This Bill is intended, not for the well-to-do classes of the community—they already have adequate educational opportunities—this Bill is intended for the labouring classes of the community. It is intended to give to the children of the people of this country an opportunity of developing to the highest possible extent the good that is in them. One of the tragedies of this war lies in the fact that young men are called upon to lay down their lives in support of a policy which has been framed by old men, and I ask you whether the time has not come for some measure of reparation; whether the time has not come when the old or the elderly men should contrive some measure of policy which will secure to the future generations of this country extended opportunities for educational development. Let us throw our minds into the future. We are sailing in very perilous waters. For the first time in the long history of this country we have encountered the enmity of a people more highly organized, more systematically educated than ourselves; and we should be living in a fool's paradise if we supposed that, contrary to all the teachings of history, this war would leave behind it no aftermath of bitterness, rancour, and competition. Our children, and our children's children, will be born into a more difficult world, and I think we shall be doing less than our duty to posterity if we do not take steps to arm them for the conflict in which they will be engaged.

In the last speech included in this collection Mr. Fisher makes the following observations about the French system :—

The aim of the French Elementary School is conceived with a clarity and pursued with a degree of force and intelligence which compel admiration. The Elementary School teacher is regarded as a missionary. In particular he is a missionary of the French language. It is his duty to uphold in every little village the purity of that wonderful instrument of human expression, to enforce its precise and correct usage, and to spread a delicate perception of its beauties as expressed in the masterpieces of national literature. And though it is always hazardous to make generalizations, my experience leads me to believe that the French Elementary School succeeds in this part of its mission, even when it is contending with an alien language like Breton, far more successfully than is the case with us.

Then again the French Primary Schools are regarded as organs for the spread of the Elementary ideas and principles of Natural Science among the great mass of people, and here again it is my impression that they achieve their mission with signal success.

And lastly, the French Elementary School teacher is regarded as a missionary of enlightened patriotism, and for this reason great stress is laid upon the teaching of History in the Normal Schools or Training Colleges of France. Indeed it is clear that the syllabus of historical instruction for these Schools has been drawn up by an historian who knows the weights and measures of the past, for it lays stress upon all the fundamental points of National History and enables the student to obtain a clear perspective of the leading factors which govern and constitute the progress of the nation to which he belongs.[1]

[1] The italics and capitals in these quotations are mine.—L.R.

VI

NATIONAL EDUCATION IN INDIA

THE BUSINESS OF THE STATE

I HAVE given these long extracts from Mr. Fisher's speeches because in my judgment they embody the fundamental principles of national education, accepted by competent authorities, all over the world. The schemes in force in different countries vary in detail, but the principles underlying them are the same. To us in India Mr. Fisher's words are of greater significance than those of educators, equally well placed, of other countries, because of our political connection with England. Here is the chief educational authority of the Empire, laying down certain principles and expounding truths which are, according to him, of general application in all self-respecting, progressively-minded communities. We, the Indians in India, are not yet free to determine our educational policy. Even with the promise of educational autonomy to the provinces, the last word will practically remain with the Imperial Government. The progress of popular education in India must, for a long time, depend on the goodwill of the British officials in charge of policies, and vested with powers over revenues and funds. The words of a British Minister of Education will be more to us in our discussions of educational policies and schemes, than those of any other authority in any other part of the world. In the region of policy the example of Great Britain is the best for our purposes, and I cannot sufficiently urge upon my countrymen the importance of using the British system as a fulcrum for the raising of educational standards in India.

This does not involve a blind imitation of British methods of education, nor does it mean that we should neglect to profit from what is being done by the other great nations of the world, especially the United States and Japan, in this department of their national life. But on the whole Britain can teach us much in this line.

In adopting Britain as our model, however, we are not bound to pass through the same processes of experiment and wastage through which she has passed in her educational evolution. It is the height of stupidity and ignorance to argue that the evolution of any nation must proceed on the same lines, as has that of those nations that are now in the vanguard of progress in the world. Why should not the younger marcher profit from the mistakes of those that have gone ahead? Why should he not avoid the wastage involved in the failures and blunders of others? Of what use is history if its warnings cannot be heeded by those to whom they are available? Let us, therefore, be on our guard against the fallacious argument that we must grow through the same mistakes, of which the others have been guilty in their growth towards freedom.

Nor does this mean that we can neglect the various stages of development through which we must pass before we can come up to the level of those who started long ago. What we require is a rational and a comprehensive scheme, taking note of the general principles which have come to be universally accepted all the world over, with special emphasis over our special needs, and with due consideration of the stage of social evolution in which we are and also of our resources.

Now we may assume that the following

general principles of national education are accepted all over the civilized world :—

1. That national education, being the surest and the most profitable national investment for gain, as well as the best and the most effectual insurance against loss, is as necessary for national safety as the military provision for its physical defence.

Among the lessons of this great war, the most important, in my judgment, is the value of education to a fighter, from a military point of view. Personal bravery and courage must, as ever, continue to be an important element in war. But even more than that, the fate and safety of nations have come to depend on the intelligence and efficiency of its fighting units. Wars are now virtually fought in schools. The numbers matter a great deal, but even much more than the numbers matter intelligence, skill, efficiency and discipline. Then, again, the efficiency of a nation does not mean merely military efficiency ; the latter is so much wound up with its economic and industrial efficiency.

Economic and industrial efficiency does not mean the mere possession of gold and silver, but the brains and capacity of the whole nation to turn that gold and silver and other raw materials into modern arms and ammunitions—ships, submarines, aeroplanes, guns and bullets are only the concrete, completed forms, containing numerous other parts, the manufacture of each of which requires technical skill of the highest order—and, last but not least, food and hospital necessities. Assuming, therefore, that security from without is the first duty of a State, popular, universal education alone can make it possible under modern conditions.

The war has conclusively established the idea that a mercenary standing army, consisting mostly of illiterate units, is an obsolete one; also that India cannot be defended by British people alone; nor can India entirely depend upon Great Britain for its supply of the sinews of war, be they arms and ammunition or the numerous other things found vital in modern warfare. If the British had foreseen this and equipped India for the inevitable struggle, they could have crushed their enemy in comparatively less time, and with greater facility. Universal education of the best modern type is, therefore, an absolute necessity for the future security of India, and the best interests of the Empire require that the human resources of the Indian Empire should be economized to the fullest extent. It is a crime to let them be wasted so flagrantly as they have been until now.

Universal popular education must be provided by the State, and should be the first charge on State revenues. Any attempt to provide for national education by private agencies and private funds is futile, and to attempt it is to attempt the impossible. Moreover, it diverts public attention from the State.

A national system of education must be provided for, enforced, financed and controlled by the nation, and in performing that function the nation must be represented by the State. It may be pointed out, as has in fact been done by Mr. B. G. Tilak, in his views on national education, that in India the nation, not being represented by the State, that function must devolve, at least for some time, on private national agencies. The remedy, in my judgment, lies in concentrating our energies on the task of converting the State into a national agency. Along with that, we can use what powers we have or are conceded to us under the new scheme, for insisting that the State provide for universal national education befitting the needs of the nation and guaranteeing in war, as well as in peace, the fullest use and development of our human and industrial resources.

National education must be provided by the nation, and whether the State is a true representative of the nation or not, it must be made to provide for it. The nation should be made conscious of this.

2. The old idea that the State was only concerned with making provision for elementary education is also gone. All over the world it is recognized that the duty of the State does not end with elementary education. The economic and industrial efficiency of the nation depends upon technical and industrial education, and that also must be provided by the State. Nor can the State ignore the necessity of higher education, for intelligent and efficient leadership depends on that.

3. Education does not consist in imparting certain amounts of book knowledge and teaching the three R's. It includes provision for the physical development of the young. It embraces a provision for the general health of the child, including feeding, if necessary, to such an extent as to ensure the fullest benefit to the child from the provision for his education made by the State.

4. In short, the duty of bringing up and educating the child with a view of helping him to become an efficient, intelligent and prudent citizen, rests with the State, and the State must be made to fulfil it. It no longer depends on the capacity or willingness of the parents.

Some great thinkers and educationalists, such as Spinoza, have maintained that the Government will, if it controls the education of the nation, " aim to restrain, rather than develop the energies of men." Kant also noticed the same difficulty.

The function of education, in the eyes of a dominant class, is to produce skilled but obedient men, as distinguished from self-thinking and self-reliant men. This theory presupposes the predominance of a particular class in the governance of the nation. Democratic ideals of government bar any such assumptions. The Imperial British Government has pledged itself to the development of responsible government on democratic lines in India. Our own ideal is the same. It may be that, so long as we do not get full responsible government, national education will more or less be under the thumb of the dominant class, but then the remedy lies mostly in our own hands.

Constant vigilance, constant agitation, constant education of the public mind, will be our duty, so long as the goal is not reached ; and when the goal is reached, our policy will be completely in our hands. Then there will be no danger of the control of education falling in hands other than those of the future Fishers of India.

At no time can or will private efforts to further education be dispensed with. Pending the development of full national government, private efforts must do a great deal of what the Government fails to do. In short, private efforts should supplement the efforts of the Government, without any pretence of supplanting it or doing what it is the latter's duty to do, and what it can, under the circumstances, be forced to do.

Private efforts, therefore, should be directed to fill up the gap left by State education, and also to supply the particular needs of particular classes with a view to bring up every class in the nation to the level of general national efficiency. It seems that education is one of the subjects under the new scheme regarding which full responsibility is going to be thrown on Provincial Legislatures. Provincial Legislatures are already legislating in some provinces at least, giving the local bodies power to declare it compulsory and to provide for it. Now, sitting at such a distance, I am unable to say much about these moves. As at present advised, I am inclined to think that this may be the proverbial vicious circle in which things move in India.

We have seen from Mr. Fisher's speeches that in England the policy is laid down by the national Government, and the bulk of funds are provided by them. For every seventeen millions sterling, provided by the local rates, the national purse has been giving sixteen millions; and the present Government, in spite of the awful strain of the war on its finances, has sanctioned the additional grant of another four millions from the national purse, thus making the national contribution twenty millions as against the seventeen millions realized from local rates.

What is going to happen in India I do not know, but of one thing I am certain in my mind, that the general outline of a scheme of national education in India must be laid down by an All-India agency, leaving the actual working out of the details to the Provincial and local bodies. This All-

India agency must have a majority of Indians on its personnel, and the policy laid down by them must be accepted by the Government, subject to the limitation of funds. What is needed is a national policy, a national scheme, and a maximum grant of national funds for the purpose, to be supplemented by Provincial taxes and local rates. Of course, the first need of the nation is more schools and more teachers. The second is good schools and good, contented teachers. The third is vocational schools, including schools for instruction in commerce and foreign languages. The fourth is technological institutes. The fifth is continuation schools. The sixth is more high schools and more universities.

I do not suggest that all this should be done simultaneously. But I believe that the bulk of the available national funds must be reserved, for some time to come, for more schools and more teachers, to give instruction to the children of the nation on national lines.

In my judgment, the first ten years of our national effort should be *mainly* devoted to (*a*) the increase of literacy; (*b*) the production of literate, skilled labour, conscious of its rights as human beings, and conscious of its rights as members of the body politic; (*c*) multiplication and training of the teachers with as great an increase in their remuneration as may be possible under the circumstances. It should be the duty of the State to provide higher technological and agricultural institutes in selected localities, in sufficient numbers to enable the nation to develop its mineral, agricultural, and industrial resources. It should be the aim of the State to fill up these institutes with Indian expert talent, which, if not forthcoming at once, should be gradually but steadily introduced as competent men, trained in foreign countries as Government scholars, or otherwise, return.

If Mr. Fisher was right, as undoubtedly he was, in saying that national education is not only an investment, but an insurance as well, I see no reason why education in India should not be provided for, pushed and furthered wherever necessary, by supplementing the amounts made available for the purpose, from the taxes and the rates, by raising additional national debt. If it was legitimate to raise money by loans for railways, and for defence and for contribution to the Imperial War Fund, why is it not legitimate to raise funds for national education and the development of essential national industries by the same means?

At this stage I may as well give another passage from one of Mr. Fisher's speeches. When addressing the manufacturers and business men of Bradford, he asked them if it does "not often happen in the management of a business that you find yourself compelled to face an additional outlay in order to get full value from the outlay that you have already made? And what is true of individual business is true of national business."

In order to get full value for the outlay which India has made on railways, canals, and the frontier defences, it is necessary to develop the intelligence, the productive power and capacity of the nation (its defensive and offensive capacity), as well as its capacity to compete with other nations on equal terms in industries and manufacture. The raising of the nation's intelligence and skill, the improvement of its physique, and the development of its earning capacity is as important, if not more so, than the development of railways, canals, and forts. Sometimes it seems to me that in India the cart has been put before the horse.

My argument is that there are certain

things which can be done only by the State and must be done by the State ; that the State should do these things even by incurring financial obligations in the nature of public debts, if the current finances are not sufficient or adequate to do them on any decent scale ; and that universal elementary education and a widespread provision for the training of teachers, and an equally widespread provision for vocational and technical education, both of the lower and the higher order, are among those things which cannot be postponed without risk of serious danger to the political safety of the nation.

These things, being provided for by the State on a scale commensurate with the needs of the nation, private effort should be unsparing to contribute toward the rest. All privately endowed colleges and academies should be allowed to develop into universities, conducting their own examinations, giving their own diplomas and conferring their own degrees. All research work in classical languages, in history and philosophy, in logic and mental and moral science, as well as in social sciences, may be left to them. The State-maintained colleges and the State universities should mainly concern themselves with scientific education, scientific development and research, and with the material development of the country. Not that the State and thc nation have no interest in the former. Oh, no ! The nation is interested in everything that develops and aids efficiency in the individual, as well as in the classes, and more so in leadership, but for the time being the above-mentioned division of labour between the State and private enterprise in education may be the best way of collaboration to economize our resources and get the best possible results from them.

VII

THE TEACHING OF PATRIOTISM

No scheme of national education in India could be complete without including the active teaching of "patriotism" and "nationalism" as a regular subject of study. In this matter we should borrow a leaf out of the book of Europe. Every European country, and the United States also, makes it a point to cultivate the spirit of patriotism and nationalism through its schools. What is being done in England and in the United States is accessible to my educated countrymen, but what has been done and is being done in France and Germany may be known to a few only. An American Professor has recently published a book[1] on the subject, from which a few extracts would, in my opinion, be useful and relevant.

Professor Scott gives a historical sketch

[1] "Patriots in the Making," by Jonathan French Scott. (Appleton's, New York, 1916.)

of the different schemes of education that have held the field in France within the last two hundred years. He begins with "France of the Ancient Regime."

Education in France under the ancient regime was neither universal nor compulsory nor free. What little of it there was, was imparted by priests and monks, and was mainly confined to the well-born boy or girl. We are told that "the little aristocrats, worldly as they were, were subject to a certain amount of religious and intellectual education. But the dancing master was conspicuous as a practical teacher. The training that he gave . . . paved the way to social success, to pensions, advancement and power at court." Then came the Revolution, the forces let loose by which were used by Napoleon for his personal glory and aggrandizement. It was his aim to make the latter identical with national glory. "What the French want," said he, "is glory and the satisfaction of their vanity; as for liberty, of that they have no conception." Thus the spirit of the era centred around the personality of the great conqueror, who could turn the dreams of the French people into realities. It was militaristic and Imperialistic, but at the same time characterized by orderliness and constructive statesmanship in home affairs. . . . From the background developed the Napoleonic system of education. All education was centralized in the Imperial University, with a grand master at the head, whom Napoleon thought to control. The Emperor aimed to make himself loved and obeyed in all the schools, securing loyalty to his despotism and to his dynasty. . . . In the primary schools the children were taught that "to honour and serve our Emperor is to honour and serve God himself." All instruction was to rest upon "the precepts of religion, of loyalty and of obedience." The result was Waterloo.

Since the fall of Napoleon I, various forces have struggled for domination over the national life of France and "hence for control over national education." The French love of glory and the national tendency to hero-worship have fought against the French devotion to reason. The monarchical principle has striven to assert itself against the growing spirit of democracy. As a rule the Church has lent its support to the monarchical principle, though "the alliance between the throne and the altar has not been so close as it was before 1789."

Though allied in principle, the Church and the State have often struggled against each other for control over education. The school was freely used by both for the strengthening of their hold on the minds of the nation, until "the tragedy of the Franco-Prussian war at once saddened and awakened the nation." From 1870 onwards, the State has striven hard to mould the mind of the nation to an acceptance of the principles and purposes of the Third Republic, and we have the authority of Professor Scott for the emphatic assertion that "the Third Republic has been a powerful and effective instrument in inculcating on the oncoming generation of Frenchmen, sentiments of patriotism and loyalty." Thus education in France from the time of Louis XIV (concludes Professor Scott) has experienced changes corresponding to changes in the government and ideals of the State.

At this stage Professor Scott emphasizes the importance which tradition and custom have had in influencing education in the European countries. "By reason of their power a given type of instruction tends to survive long after the forces that gave birth to it have ceased to be vital." Thus it was that the classics maintained in the nineteenth century a position in the English public schools entirely disproportionate to their value to society. Similarly, a new social force may long knock at the door of the school before being allowed to enter. Thus we find that the system of every country has been more or less encumbered with survivals.

With the growth of national consciousness, however, education has tended to become a political instrument, the study of it almost a branch of political science. This is true of almost every country in Europe and America.

In every living community inspired by national ideas and ambitions the national consciousness expresses itself through the school as perhaps through no other institution. From a study of the schools of Europe. the methods followed by them, and the text-books used therein, one can very well study the growth of national consciousness and national purpose, in the different countries of Europe and America.

In giving this synopsis of Professor Scott's introductory chapter, I have travelled beyond the purpose I had set before me in the opening page of this chapter. I have done so intentionally, in order to point out to my countrymen the importance of the school in the development and progress of national consciousness, and how necessary it is to avoid encumbering our education with survivals. The best use of history is to avoid the mistakes through which other nations have cleared their way before us. To repeat the same, in the face of the clear verdict of history, is to refuse to listen to the warnings of the latter and be guilty of unpardonable pugnacity.

For the last fifty years, ever since the disaster of Sedan (in 1870), the French nation and the French Government have been very active in the teaching of patriotism to their boys and girls. Gambetta placed national education even above compulsory military service and a more rigorous application of the principle of national sovereignty. "This land must be rebuilt," said he, "its customs renovated, the evil which is the cause of all our ills, ignorance, must be made to disappear; there is but one remedy, the education of all." "In moulding the psychology of defence against aggression it was not considered enough, of course, that the state should stand sponsor for the education of every boy and girl between the age of six and thirteen years." It was considered necessary that the ideals of the nation be unified and the children of the nation be led to realize the gravity of their country's problems. In other words, the systematic inculcating of " A staunch and true devotion to the Fatherland, sufficient to weather any crisis," became a vital principle of education in schools. " Therefore direct instruction in patriotism has been given in the schools, which has resolved chiefly round the following points : (1) the love of France ; (2) the military spirit and the obligatory service ; and (3) the duty of cultivating physical courage. Furthermore (4) the children have learned to know that taxation is necessary to support the army ; (5) they have been given some definite information in regard to the state of the national defence ; and (6) certain writers have pointed out to them the perils of depopulation in a country menaced by increasingly powerful neighbours."

A few extracts from the text-books will show how these objects have been attained. Under the head of " La Patrie," one author writes :—

Do you know what the fatherland is ? It is the house where your mother has carried you in her arms. It is the lawn on which you play your joyous games. It is the school where you receive yo first instruction. It is the town hall where floats the flag of France. It is the cemetery where your ancestors rest. It is the clock which you see again with new joy on each return to the village. It is the fields which bear the traces of the labours of your fathers. It is the hills, the mountains which you have so many times climbed.

Men of the same country are *compatriots*; they form a great family, a nation.

The thirty-seven million inhabitants of France constitute the *French family*. They have the same history, the same joys, the same hopes. They sorrow over the humiliation of their common Fatherland, and take pride in her prosperity; they share her fortune, good or bad.

Another text-book says: "Love of France constitutes the road to happiness; more than that, it is the first of duties."

"The Fatherland," says another, "is the nation which you should love, honour and serve with all the strength of your body, with all the energy and all the devotion of your soul."

In a little poem a father thus counsels his son:—

Be son and brother to the end,
My joy and happiness enhance,
But lad, be sure, 'fore all else
You place the love of France.

Now, there is nothing extraordinary in all these extracts: we find equally noble and inspiring sentiments in our national songs. The " Bande Mátaram," the " Amar Desh," and the " Hindustan Hamárá," all breathe the same spirit. The point is that they should be taught systematically by text-books and by word of mouth, in schools and in school hours. " There are people," says Compayre, the writer of one of these text-books, " who say, ' One does not learn to love one's country.' They deceive themselves," he retorts; " one learns to love one's country as one learns everything else. Nor is it sufficient to love one's country. It is also necessary to know why one loves her. Only through such knowledge can patriotism rest on a sound basis."

Thus by instruction the ideal of devotion to the Fatherland is implanted and fostered in the hearts of the youth of France; and upon this foundation is reared the superstructure of the various duties which patriotism entails.

Be it said to the credit of the French text-book writers that they do not fail to caution their youthful readers " against the spirit of chauvinism, warning them, for example, against too keen a suscepti to slight and insults, and condemning such aggressions as those of Francis I against Italy, Louis XIV against Holland, and Napoleon against Europe."

In another text-book the writer advises his youthful readers to be ever ready for all emergencies. "Be ready," says he, "when 'the day' arrives, be prepared to endure hunger, thirst and cold for the sake of the Fatherland. Be ready to die rather than abandon your post."

"Bravery is courage in battle," says another man. "In war, courage and steadiness are necessary every minute. To march in weather icy cold or burning hot, often with wounded feet, with chilblains, to lie on the damp earth, to suffer thirst and hunger; all this must be endured gaily. Those who complain are bad comrades, for discouragement is contagious. . . . Keep cool under fire, and we shall be invincible." It does not require any argument to prove that such teachings play an important part in the formation of the national psychology. They justify the programme of compulsory military training and the discipline that accompanies it, as without this latter "courage, enthusiasm and self-sacrifice would be powerless against hostile" forces organized and trained.

The French supplement their lessons in love of country and bravery by regular instruction in regard to national defences and taxation. Every French child knows by heart the frontiers of his country and what provision there is for defending it against possible invaders. He also begins to realize the necessity of contributions to the National Treasury, for the purposes of national defence. The unique bravery, dash, courage and selflessness with which the French have faced the Germans in the Great War was the result of this systematic training which has formed a regular feature of national education in France for the last fifty years. Over and above this general education about patriotism the French leaders have also been inculcating hostility towards Germany as an article of national faith. This hostility was embodied in the word *revanche,* or reprisal. In the war of 1870 the French lost heavily, and had to cede two of their richest provinces, Alsace and Lorraine, to Germany. The idea of regaining these lost provinces was never abandoned; hence the doctrine of *revanche.* "Geographies, histories, readers and manuals of moral and civic instruction have played their part in fostering a psychology of hostility toward Germany." "But in spite of it, it may be questioned," adds Professor Scott, "whether the teaching of *revanche* ever rose to the dignity of a national policy." It must be noted, however, that the dark and sombre pictures of Teutonism drawn for the purposes of *revanche* were not altogether unrelieved by the light of praise. "Certain qualities of the Germans the French lad is called upon to admire and presumably to imitate. The perseverance and the spirit of discipline by which Prussia has become powerful are commended; so also is the Teutonic ardour for work."

Loyalty to republican principles and ideas of democracy was the third plank in the French platform of national education. This was made necessary by the reactionary monarchist movements that disfigure the history of France after the Revolution of 1789.

Among the other forces which have contributed to French national consciousness in the nineteenth century, have been the teaching of patriotic history as distinguished from scientific history and of nationalism as against pacifism. On these points, however, there has never been anything like unanimity, either among French educators or among the statesmen and publicists of France. The teaching of patriotism in Germany has been of a more aggressive and ambitious nature. Theirs was not a psychology of defence nor one of loyalty to democratic ideals that needed to be cultivated. It included a programme of world conquest, militarily, politically, economically as well as culturally. The German schools promulgated loyalty to the emperor. The French laid emphasis on efficiency, unity, pride of race and birth, and the Germans on the necessity of maintaining the monarchical form of government and of strengthening the tie between the nation and the throne. The German throne stood for absolutism supported by efficiency.

In England and the United States, the teaching of patriotism has been more indirect than direct. Worship of the flag, respect for the National Anthem, the sense of pride in the Empire, etc., have been fostered by means of patriotic teaching of history and geography, and also more by social processes than by direct pedagogical methods.

Among the Asiatic nations, Japan and China are now following in the footsteps of the Europeans in making the teaching of patriotism a regular feature of their schemes of national education. Can we in India neglect this ?

VIII

THE TEACHING OF PATRIOTISM (*concluded*)

THE teaching of patriotism in India and its place in the scheme for national education must revolve round the following points:

(1) Love of India as a whole, as distinguished from love of village, town, city or province. There is enough in both the Hindu and Mohammedan literature to strengthen this sentiment and to bring it in line with the beautiful and ever-inspiring lines of Scott.

I am sure Indian Nationalists do not want to set up an aggressive nationalism of the kind which will breed contempt or hatred of other nations. The idea that love of one's country necessarily involves hatred of others, or even indifference to the welfare of the rest of mankind, is absolutely fallacious and mischievous, and should be combated through and through. We love our country because that, and that alone, can enable us to ascend to the heights of humanity.

The justification of this characteristic, says Sir Charles Waldstein, lies in its efficiency in the social life of man.[1]

"As the forces of consanguinity act upon members of a family and a home, so with the citizens of a State, the physical and practical conditions of national life and of the native country are the true training ground for the most effective higher moral idealism, ending in the love of mankind. . . . Not merely in thought, but also in the emotional life of man, the world of feelings and of passions, which are the most direct and effective sources of action, this love of country, this true patriotism has the most ennobling influence."

Vague, undefined, indeterminate cosmopolitanism is often a disguise for gross selfishness and a life of sensuous inactivity. We cannot do better than caution the younger generations of Indians against the fallacies of the cult of vague cosmopolitanism. Some time ago, when addressing a meeting of a Cosmopolitan Club attached to one of the famous Universities of America (Columbia), the present writer took occasion to point out that while cosmopolitanism meant some-

[1] "Patriotism, National and International," by Sir Charles Waldstein, p. 143. (Longmans, 1917.)

thing noble when coming from the mouth of an Englishman or an American, in the mouth of a Hindu and a Chinese (there were Hindus and Chinese in the gathering) it means only an attempt to escape the duties which patriotism lays on them. While I respect the former, I added, for their cosmopolitanism, I despise the latter for their lack of patriotism. For them it will be time to become cosmopolitan after they have cultivated patriotism and raised their respective countries to the level of other independent, self-conscious, self-respecting nations.

Mazzini's famous dictum on cosmopolitanism and nationalism should never be forgotten. Intense and devoted patriotism is quite consistent with the love of humanity. We should spare no pains to point out the co-operative nature of our patriotism and the analytical dangers of a loose cosmopolitanism. There are only a few men in the world, if there be any, who can be true cosmopolitans without being true patriots. There is no such thing as International patriotism, unless the expression is used in the sense that our patriotism must take cognizance of our International duties and must not violate the rights of others who are not our nationals.

Text-books for the primary schools should be free from discussions of Nationalism and Internationalism. They should inculcate the love of India, of Indian rivers, Indian hills, Indian landscape, Indian scenes, in choice, simple language. Is there any place on earth which is more beautiful and more sublime than our Himalaya ? Is there any river which is more majestic and inspiring than Ganga or Brahmaputra or Narbada or even Sindh ? Are there any cities which in their natural situation and in their past historic traditions can excel Srinagar, Benares, Allahabad, Patna, Lahore, Bombay, Karachi, Madras, Delhi, and Dacca ? In short, in physical features, natural scenery, fertility of soil, productive climate, we have everything in our country to be proud of.

Among domestic and useful animals, what country on earth produces more beautiful cows and bullocks ? Our horses and camels, dogs and cats, sheep and goats, are inferior to none. We have noble trees, the noble *pipal*, the great *chanár*, the tall poplar, the sacred bo, and many others. We grow fruits which in flavour and delicacy, sweetness and taste, are superior to any other in the world. The kingly mango, the guava, the orange, the banana, the mangosteen, the grape, the melon; oh, how impossible it is to count them! There is no one country on earth which produces fruits of such variety and of such high quality. Corns and cereals, pulses and oil seeds, vegetables and roots—the variety and taste of these is simply amazing. The text-books meant for little children should, in suitable language, dilate on the beauties and the bounties of our country.

Patriotism, however, does not include only the material and the physical aspects of a country. "It includes all that Renan has called *l'âme d'une nation*, the more delicate shadings of feelings, such as piety for the past, admiration and love of the heroic figures in the history of the nation, and its great achievements; love of language, community of tradition, laws and customs, and all that gives individual character to the civilization of each nation."

This leads us to the second point around which our teaching of patriotism should revolve, viz.:—

(2) The love of the nation as a whole, regardless of the various religious creeds and castes into which it is internally divided.

Every Indian child should be taught in so many words that every human being who is born in India, or of Indian parents, or who has made India his or her home, is a compatriot, a brother or a sister, regardless of colour, creed, caste or vocation. The diversity of race, religion and language is often exploited by the foreigner as a pretext to deny us the status and the privileges of a nation. Now it should be made absolutely clear to every Indian youth that in India there is no such thing as the conflict of races. No Indian, Hindu or Mohammedan, ever attaches any importance to his racial origin or to the racial origin of the rest of his countrymen. *There is no country on the face of the globe which has a pure race.* The sons of man have so freely mixed and mingled in the past, that racial distinctions are only a matter of imagination or conjecture. More often than not they are a cloak for political dominance and economic exploitation.

All these ethnological pretensions and passions—and this is one of the distinctive features of the more modern conflict of "races"—are based upon the achievements and results of modern ethnological study, the youngest and *least accurate* of modern sciences. In federation with the revised study of philology, comparative religion and anthropology, the *ethnological politician and agitator* found a fertile field, especially for internal disintegration and antagonism, in the inner life of modern States (*in most cases neither consciously nor unconsciously quite free from consideration of material interest and greeds*) in the antagonism between Aryanism and Semitism.[1]

It is the anti-Jewish sentiment to which Sir Charles Waldstein expressly refers in this quotation. But the mischief which these theories are working is not confined to " internal disintegration and antagonism in the inner life of modern States " ; it extends to the wider and extended sphere of relations between one nation and another. The cries of the " yellow peril " and the " black peril " also are traceable to the same causes. It is the desire of political domination and economic exploitation that is at the bottom of these cries, and it is a matter of sincere joy that some of the most eminent sociologists of the age are earnestly combating these vicious theories. Professor Todd ascribes modern race boasting and strutting to " ignorance " and to deliberate fostering of imperialism and dynastic pretensions ; as well as to " the headiness " which comes from the new wine of quick and easy success. He examines with some details the extra-

[1] " Patriotism, National and International," by Sir Charles Waldstein, p. 133. The italics are mine.—L. R.

vagant and foolish claims of the tribe of Bernhardis and Chamberlains.[1] The following observations on page 284 of his book are worth being quoted :—

> Owing to the internationalizing of human activities, an international osmosis, so to speak, the concept of race is of diminishing importance and may disappear from the focus of men's thought and passions. Hence it turns out that the real selective forces in complex societies are economic, or moral, or psychological or educational, but not ethnic.

Later on, he concludes that " the inevitableness of race conflict is still only a hypothesis ; rather let us say, superstitious survival in our world mores."

In India there is no race conflict. Hindu and Mussulman and Christian are all a racial " mix-up." The Mussulman descendants of Persian, Afghan, Turkaman, Mogul and Arab invaders have a great deal of Aryan blood in their veins and the Hindu descendants of the Aryans have a great deal of Mongolian blood. The Anglo-Indians of India, too, have all these veins. It is stupid and mischievous to talk of race conflict in India. Mother India knows and recognizes no race distinctions.

[1] Houston Stewart Chamberlain is also German.

But that there is a religious conflict in India cannot be denied. Even that conflict is more artificial than real, manufactured quite recently by interested parties. In the remote past, there was once a conflict between the Hindus and the Buddhists; then there were occasional conflicts between the Hindus and the Mussulmans. It was almost dying out when it was revived by political agitators and schemers on both sides, under the impetus of outside influences. Even when *bona fide,* it was due to false ideas of religious nationalism and communal patriotism. Even that bitter critic of the Indian Nationalists, Mr. William Archer, has admitted that before the "British established themselves in India, Muhammadan princes ruled over Hindu subjects, and Hindu princes over Muhammadan subjects, with very tolerable impartiality of rule or mis-rule. And the same is true in the native states of to-day, not merely as a result of British over-lordship. At no time since the days of Aurangzeb has either religion seriously tried to over-power and cast out the other." Did even Aurangzeb ever do it? A careful scanning of the history of India for the last thousand years, from the invasion of Abdul Qasim up to the disappearance of the last vestige of Mogul sovereignty shows nothing which by any stretch of imagination may be compared with the conflict between Roman Catholicism and Protestantism which raged in Europe for over four centuries. Is there anything in Indian history which can be cited as parallel to the massacre of St. Bartholomew's Day in France, or to the orgies committed by the rival sects in Holland, Spain, Italy, Germany, and even Great Britain and Ireland, in their frenzied attempts to extirpate one another?

The general massacres ordered by Tamerlane and Nadir Shah made no distinction between Hindus and Mohammedans. The long trains of slaves taken away by Mahmud and others of that period are occurrences of a period when there were very few or no Mohammedans in India. There is no authentic record of Aurangzeb having ordered any general massacre of the Hindus in any part of the country. There was some persecution of the Mohammedans by the Sikhs by way of reprisal (*revanche*), but it was confined to the Punjab, and even there it was by no means general. Hindus and Mohammedans have come to realize that India is the country of all of them, that their future prosperity and progress depends on their unity, and that religion is a matter of individual faith and taste; and that with the common civil life of the country, religion does not and should not interfere. But it must form an important part of the active teaching of patriotism in India to impress on the minds of young children the fact of their common country, of their common political and economic interests, of their common history and of their common destiny. Text-books of patriotism should take special cognizance of this branch of the subject and insist on the essential unity of Hindus and Mussulmans as also of Christians and Buddhists, Parsees and Sikhs and Jains. These text-books should take particular notice of the best and glorious achievements of both the Hindus and the Mohammedans.

To be Indians, first, last, and all the time, in all political and economic matters and in our relations with non-Indians, must be taught to our boys and girls by written and printed lessons as well as by word of mouth. It is a necessary and a vital article of faith in the religion of patriotism that we must teach to our boys and girls. Even denominational schools and colleges and universities *must* include it in their curricula of studies. Thank God, the spirit of unity is abroad in India, and we can safely build upon it. But it will be folly to ignore the counteracting forces. We must meet them by active, deliberate and well-concerted plans. Complete success may not attend our efforts speedily, but come it must and, by the grace of God, it will.

The teaching of Hindu-Mohammedan unity can be greatly facilitated by the writing of special and carefully worded theses on the lives of our national heroes. Lives of Shivaji, Partap and Govind Singh, as well as those of Akbar, Sher Shah and Shah Jahan must be carefully written. They should contain no untruths; they should be scrupulously true, but written from a broad, patriotic and national point of view. They should be a composite production of patriotic and scientific history. Hindus should learn to take pride in the achievements of Mohammedan heroes, saints, and writers, and the Mohammedans in those of the Hindus.

If Mother India is proud of a Nanak, she is also proud of a Chisti. If she had an Asoka, she had an Akbar too. If she had a Chaitanya, she had Kabir also. If she had a Harsha, she had a Sher Shah too. If she had a Vikramaditya, she had a Shah Jahan also. If she had a Mohammedan Ala Uddin Khilji and a Mohammedan Tuglaq, she had their Hindu prototypes as well. For every Hindu hero, she can cite a Mohammedan hero. If she is proud of a Todar Mal, she is equally proud of Abul Fazl. She can as well be proud of her *Khusroes*, *Faizís*, *Gálibs*, *Zauqs*, *Ferishtás* and *Gánimats* (I wonder if *Gánimat* was not a Hindu), as she can be of *Válmíki*, *Kálídás*, *Tulsídás*, *Rám Dás*, *Chánd Násim* and *Gobind Singh*. Even we modern Indians can be as well proud of a *Hálí*, an *Iqbál*, a *Moháni* as of *Tagore*, *Roy* and *Harish Chandra*. We are as proud of *Syed Ahmed Khan* as of *Ram Mohan Roy* and *Dayananda*.

As regards caste, even Archer admits that in spite of caste Hinduism is and will remain a mighty bond of union. Hindus and Mussulmans must unite to remove all internal divisions based on caste. All social barriers must be removed and the school, the college, the court and the council must be open temples for all to enter and worship, regardless of caste, colour and creed. Even in other social relations, the line of differentiation should be thinned with a view to its ultimate extinction, till religious beliefs become a matter of individual personal faith.

This will not come of itself; we should pledge ourselves to it, by making it a subject of study for our children, in all national schools and colleges—nay, even in denominational schools and colleges.

(3) The third part of our course for the teaching of patriotism must deal with our relations with the State. The promise of responsible self-government within the Empire makes us free to include our obligations to the State in this course. If the Empire treats us on terms of equality, we shall be true and loyal to the Empire, and faithfully discharge our obligations towards it.

The announcement made by the Secretary of State for India in August, 1917, must be made the foundation of this part of the scheme of studies. The constitution of the Government of India should form a part of the curriculum of studies with full freedom to the teachers to explain by what processes and by what qualifications we could have it improved along democratic lines and what we have to do in order to win complete self-government. Advanced students in high schools, colleges and universities should be absolutely unhampered and free to discuss politics and economics.

The German theory of the supremacy of the State over the nation must be repudiated, and the future citizen should be trained to think that the nation is superior to and in every way the master of the State. She determines the form of the State and is free to change it as, in her corporate capacity, and by her corporate will, she wishes to.

In short, our loyalty must be rational, reasoned and sincere. Let me make it clear that any attempt to enforce the teaching of loyalty to the established British Government in India as such, without pointing out the road to make it truly national and truly democratic, will end in fiasco. The analogy of Germany does not apply. The Indians must feel that their loyalty is voluntary, and an outcome of their conscious desire to remain a part of the British Commonwealth on terms of equality with the other parts of the Empire.

IX

THE PLACE OF PHYSICAL EDUCATION

EVERY great man, British or non-British, Indian or foreign, has told us that the children of to-day are the citizens of to-morrow, and that in order to have good citizens (good physically, morally and intellectually), the body politic should take good care of its children. It is now freely recognized all the world over, that the community and the State have as much, if not even greater, interest in the health and moral and mental equipment of the children of the community as the family wherein they are born. No one has proposed to lessen or belittle the responsibility of the parents, as it would be extremely demoralizing and suicidal to do so. Every normally healthy man and woman has a duty towards the race which can be fulfilled only by begetting children. The Hindus have characterized it as a debt (*rin*), which has to be paid by every healthy individual before he or she dies, in order to ensure him or her a desirable form of re-incarnation. The modern world is also gradually but surely coming to that viewpoint, subject to conditions and limitations necessary in the interest of the race.

If it is necessary that every normal man and woman should raise one or more children, in order to perpetuate the race, it is also necessary that the children so raised should be healthy and capable of contributing to the general progress of humanity. Defective persons are only a drag on the race, and involve a tragic waste of human powers, energies and potentialities.

Descending from the race to the nation, the importance of children—of healthy, vigorous and potentially resourceful and powerful children—to the latter is self-evident. The children of a nation are its greatest asset. They represent its capital, upon the wise and skilful investment of which depends its prosperity—nay, even its existence and continuance. All the civilized nations of the world have accepted this truth, and are vying with each other in building their present and future position among the peoples of the world. They are doing all that follows the acknowledgment of such a truth. Huge sums of money are being spent on public health and public education.

The two tests by which the efficiency of a Government is judged are the lowness of the death-rate among its citizens and the provision made for public education. The health of the individual is no longer his or her own concern. It is the concern of the whole community—the same is true as regards mental equipment. The health and mental equipment of every unit of the body politic are matters of national concern. The present and future interests of the nation require that every one of its citizens, male or female, should possess the maximum amount of health and the maximum of developed intelligence, possible under the circumstances, to enable it to hold its own among the peoples of the world.

In matters of health and education, individual freedom is not recognized. As far as possible no one can be permitted to be ignorant and diseased. Of course, no amount of solicitude on the part of the State can prevent a person from contracting disease if he is careless enough to be indifferent about it. It is, however, the duty of the State to lay down the minimum of health and mental equipment which it requires from its citizens and, for that purpose, it makes education compulsory, and lays down certain regulations for private and public health. With the progress of civilization, this minimum is being raised to a possible maximum in every community.

The State not only concerns itself with the education and health of its existing citizens, it goes further and regulates the birth and the training of its future members too. From this motive proceeds the ever increasing interest which the various Governments in the world are showing in the study of eugenics, in making different kinds of provision for motherhood, including their care and comfort during pregnancy and confinement, as also in providing from public funds for the care and education of children from birth up to puberty. The health of school children and their physical development for a healthy, vigorous, alert, resourceful manhood, is thus becoming a matter of supreme importance every day.

We, in India, are guilty of a criminal waste of our human resources by our dilatoriness in recognizing the supreme importance and urgency of the problems of public health and public education. While a certain amount of national awakening is observed in the attitude of the nation to the problems of education, it is not yet generally recognized that a provision for the health of school children is a necessary item of the programme if education is to be effective. Every educated Indian knows how much he has suffered in health, vitality and energy by a one-sided education which took no notice of the physical requirements of his body.

The premature deaths of our leading men are a constant subject of lamentation in our press. But the number of lives lost or smothered or ruined during the period of adolescence or before attaining a recognized position in society, is known only to the gods. Nobody counts them. Millions die every year of the harm done to their systems by neglect of their health during school and college days. Medical examination of school children has, of late, been much talked of in India, but the progress made in that direction is very slight. The results so far obtained have revealed an appalling condition of things, yet the awakening of the public mind has not been sufficiently marked to force attention to it.

As to the adoption of means to protect the health of school children, no one seems to think that the question is at all one of immediate importance. The two things which are of the greatest importance to every human being are health and ability to earn a decent livelihood. Both are criminally neglected in India. We have every year about a hundred thousand young men engaged in mastering Milton, Shakespeare, Southey, Shelley, Kalidasa and Firdausi, who have never been told, either at home or at school, how to cultivate an erect posture, how to take care of their bodies, hands, legs, noses, eyes, teeth, ears, organs, muscles and nerves. They know nothing about the hygiene of living, of housing, of food, of dress and of mating. The curriculum of studies takes no cognizance of these things, nor of those which provide recreation and amusement of a healthy and edifying character.

Nine hundred and ninety-nine out of a thousand graduates of Indian schools and colleges grow to manhood without any knowledge or taste for music. Hardly one in a hundred graduates of our universities can be confidently said to be possessed of normal health. We have had numerous reports about " how to improve the teaching of English," and some relating to other subjects, such as mathematics, science, law, etc.; we have had the reports of Commissions on Industrial Education, but so far we have done nothing to study the physical condition of our school population and to find out what we could do to secure an improvement in their health and physique.

Before me lies a small Bulletin of the United States Bureau of Education (No. 50, of 1917) on the subject of "Physical Education in Secondary Schools." It embodies the recommendations of the Commission on the Reorganization of Secondary Education in the United States, a perusal of which will be of more practical use to our educational leaders, teachers and students than volumes of high-class English and Sanskrit poetry. The report of the Committee on physical education is published in this Bulletin with a preface written by the Chairman of the Commission. It opens with the following observation:—

The Commission on the Reorganization of Secondary Education recognizes health as fundamental among the objectives of secondary education. The importance and essential scope of health education are summarized as follows:

During the period of secondary education health needs cannot be neglected without serious danger to the individual and to the race. The secondary school should, therefore, provide health instruction, inculcate health habits, organize an effective programme of physical activities, regard health needs in planning work and play, and co-operate with home and community in safeguarding and promoting health interests.

To carry out such a programme it is necessary to arouse the public to recognize that the health needs of young people are of vital importance to society, to secure teachers competent to ascertain and meet the needs of individual pupils and able to inculcate in the entire student body a love for clean sport, to furnish adequate equipment for physical activities, and to make the school building, its rooms, and surroundings conform to the best standards of hygiene and sanitation.

The report begins by stating the problem in a few lucid sentences from which I make the following extracts :—

In the new civilization, one of the most important problems of the high school, and the central problem of physical education, is how to secure and conserve health. This is becoming more and more a community problem.

The schools have been slow to adjust their programme to the changed needs of the pupils and the community. Pupils no longer go to school three months in the winter to learn to read, write, and cipher, securing their vocational skill and bodily power during the other nine months. They go to school nine months and are idle the other three, because the opportunities for developing vocational skill and bodily endurance have been taken away from them with the removal of industry from the home to the factory

The school must accept the new conditions of this industrial age and provide adequate opportunity for bodily exercise related to vocational skill and for the fundamental bodily exercises related to health.

Medicine has made splendid strides during recent years in decreasing the mortality due to zymotic diseases. The diseases which are increasing, those of the nervous system, are more inimical to the organic health of those who survive than are the infectious diseases. Insanity is on the increase. Dr. Harris, formerly United States Commissioner of Education, as early as 1891 wrote:

"Our civilization is so bent on the conquest of nature and the production of wealth that it perpetually strains its supply of nervous energy and produces disaster. Here is the special problem of our time for hygiene to meet—How to restore and conserve nervous energy. There are three factors here: First, the one of food and its proper assimilation; second, the factor of sleep and rest; third, the factor of exercise, muscular and mental."

While the increase in nervous diseases is rightly charged to a failure of bodily adjustment to the environment of the new civilization, to the saving of the weaker ones who formerly died in infancy, and to the greater strain of modern conditions, and although the number so classified is due in part to better diagnosis, it is a just indictment to say that the public schools have materially helped to augment conditions which lead to these diseases. It is not enough that the schools should not continue to increase the tendency to these diseases; they should in a constructive way assist in the necessary health adjustments of the pupils in city and country. It is the firm belief of this commission that the modern public high school owes a duty to the health of the adolescent youth of this country as a fundamental element of education. It is the belief of this commission that this duty is possible of fulfilment.

So far the public school has pre-empted the field of health education without occupying it. Theoretically, educators believe that health is more important than quantity of knowledge; practically, they seldom act upon the belief. The programme of studies has not been adjusted to meet the changed needs of the pupils. The present arrangements for physical activity can be looked upon only as palliative measures in that they give some relief from the school desk. They are essentially of negative character, aiming to minimize harmful influences. *The work of the school calls primarily for the functional activity of the higher centres of the central nervous system.* It fails to emphasize the principal positive hygienic factor in that it disregards the motor activities related to the lower nervous centres controlling circulation, respiration, nutrition, and elimination. Besides, it neglects an important phase of education in that it minimizes to the vanishing point those motor activities related to good carriage, motor presence, motor personality, and motor consciousness. The attainment of adequate motor control is impossible with the present equipment and time allotment.

Health is definitely related to the vigorous use of the big muscles of the trunk and legs. Instruction should be given in exercises and games which will bring into play these large fundamental muscles, and should be pushed far enough to stimulate circulation, respiration, and perspiration. Methods of study should be devised which will allow more freedom and bodily movement even in academic work.

This is followed by a definite programme:

The health needs of the high school pupil call for the following health programme:

I. A careful health examination which should include:
   A. Medical inspection.
   B. Mental examination.
   C. Physical examination.

II. A healthful environment in home and school.

III. Instruction in health problems.

IV. Physical activity.
   A. Equipment, minimum requirement.
   B. Amount and kind, minimum requirement.
   C. Kind of exercise.

V. School credit.

I. HEALTH EXAMINATION.

The first step in the health programme is to discover how nature has endowed the individual. It must ascertain by examination the physical and mental endowment and capacity for activity.

A. *Medical inspection.*—The English and American medical inspection methods are well outlined in such books as Cornell's "Health and Medical Inspection of School Children," Kelynack's "Examination of Schools and Scholars," Newmayer's "Medical Inspection of Schools." The administrative methods are presented in Rapeer's "School Health Administration." The objects of medical inspection have been the detection of infectious diseases, of physical defects in the pupil, and the improvement of the sanitary condition of the schoolroom. The medical inspector should co-operate with the physical instructor in the correction of physical defects and with the regular teacher or the trained psychologist in the diagnosis and treatment of mental defects.

B. *Mental examination.*—The mental examination should seek to ascertain the mental health of the pupil and his nervous and mental constitution. The health of an individual depends in large measure upon a normal central nervous system, and upon his attitude of mind toward his work. The time of entering the junior high school (seventh grade) is the most critical time in adolescence. At this time the constitution is particularly liable to nervous difficulties, as most neuroses either develop at this time, or lay their insidious hold then upon the individual, to develop later. Much stress in modern psychology is laid upon the necessity of correlating the programme of the pupil with his dominant interest. In the junior high school he is offered a choice of subjects for the first time. The proper adjustment of his programme is often related closely to his nervous health, and data for this adjustment should include the results obtained by mental tests.

It is probably unnecessary that critical mental examinations should be given to every pupil. It is, however, necessary to give such an examination to the subnormal and the supernormal pupil. For the other pupils an examination of their grades in their studies, correlated with their grades in physical education and manual training, will give a very fair index of their nervous and mental health and constitution, and will give data on which to base an all-round programme for their high-school courses. In correlating the grades of the pupils special care should be taken to make sure that the marks represent capacity rather than mere attendance and good deportment. Care should be exercised, too, in differentiating between manual training and physical education. Manual training calls for the use of the small muscles of the eye and the hand, and in a light degree, the big muscles of the arms, legs, and trunk. Manual skill of the small muscles represents, in general, health of the fine neuromuscular mechanisms. In physical education the large muscles of the arms, legs, and trunk should be used vigorously. Good grades in this work would represent fundamental health with organic, neural and muscular capacity.

In terms of the physical education grades, pupils who are fond of physical activities, excel in them, and are leaders in games and sports, as a rule possess good central nervous systems. The extreme type of these pupils, the athletes, need to be curbed in their sport. The athletic scholarship rules are made largely for their benefit, to repress too great attention to sport, and to stimulate scholarship. On the other hand the pupil who has little physical skill and takes no interest in games and sports usually lacks organic vigour. In the extreme type of these pupils is the recluse and the bookworm. It is especially in this class than an unstable nervous system may be expected. If their education is confined to a purely intellectual education, it will be at the expense particularly of the organic centres of the nervous system, related to circulation, respiration, and nutrition.

A well-balanced course for each individual is the ideal. A mental examination, with all the modern methods for the subnormal and the supernormal, and a careful examination of the grades of the average pupil, with special reference to his work in physical education and manual training upon entering the high school, will aid materially in a wise selection of high-school courses.

C. *Physical examination.*—The physical examination calls for a study of the growth and physique of the pupil, and a close correlation of the conditions found with the physical activity prescribed. The examination should include such vital problems as eyesight, hearing, growth in height and weight, bodily strength, lung capacity, cardiac efficiency. All these factors should be correlated with the adolescent maturity of the pupils and their scholarship. They are in themselves indices of mental capacity and maturity. The programmes of the schools should recognize and use these findings.

Periods of rapid growth in height and weight precede growth in strength and endurance. Vigorous big-muscle exercise should be the rule during this period. Over-exercise particularly should be avoided.

A clean-cut differentiation should be made between chronological age and physiological maturity. Both the physical examination and the physical efficiency tests should serve as aids in properly grading the health activities. Detailed studies on various phases of these problems have been made by Baldwin, Boaz, Crampton, Hughlings-Jackson, Foster, Godin, Hall, Marro, McCurdy, Stewart, and Whipple.

Medical, mental, and physical examinations should

be correlated with each other and with the general programme of the pupil. Heretofore the examinations have been conducted partly by the medical inspectors, partly by trained psychologists, and partly by the director of physical education, without correlation between them.

II. A Healthful Environment in Home and School.

A healthful environment should include a home with adequate food for healthy growth, together with sleeping and living rooms which follow at least the minimum regulations of size, light, and ventilation. It should include a schoolroom properly ventilated, with temperature never above 70 degrees, and preferably between 63 and 65 degrees F., provided a normal relative humidity of approximately 50 per cent. and adequate air movement are maintained. The schoolroom should be supplied with proper natural and artificial lighting systems, and the walls should be so coloured as to reduce eye-strain. The text-books should have size of type and width of line suitable for the proper position of the pupil at the desks. The desks should be arranged to save eye-strain and decrease poor posture and deformity. The floors and walls should be kept free from dust. The schedule should be arranged as far as possible to increase body movements and decrease nervous strain. This may best be accomplished by having pupils change from room to room and by alternating kinds of work. In addition, 3-minute setting-up drills may with profit be used two or three times per day.

III. Instruction in Health Problems.

The pupils should be given instruction in : (*a*) The practical elementary problems which concern their health ; as, for example, diet, care of the teeth, sex, sleep, exercise, and bathing in school and at home. (*b*) The general conditions related to health, as room temperature, ventilation, dust, school seating, and posture. (*c*) The public-health problems, like sewage disposal, milk and water supplies, and general control of infectious diseases.

Every pupil in the high school should be acquainted with elementary health problems in his environment. Direct application should be made to home, school, and community conditions. Definite reports of health conditions which test the powers of observation should be required. The examinations should test both the knowledge and the health habits of the pupils in home and school.

IV. Physical Activities.

A. *Equipment* (*minimum requirements*).—The equipment for physical activities in the public high school should include gymnasiums, showers, dressing-rooms, playgrounds, and, if kept in a thoroughly hygienic condition, swimming pools. Abundant sunlight and adequate ventilation and air movement are essential elements in making the building a hall of health. The location of the gymnasium in an annex is strongly recommended, as it allows better hygienic conditions and permits greater freedom.

(1) *Gymnasiums.*—In large schools of more than 600 pupils there should be two gymnasiums, one for boys and one for girls, each large enough for a class

of 50, that is, 60 by 80 feet. If we assume that each class contains 50 pupils; that the school day contains seven 45-minute periods; that a plan of overlapping 90-minute periods is adopted, making seven gymnasium periods per day, then one such gymnasium will provide two double gymnasium periods per week for 875 pupils, and the two gymnasiums will provide for 1,750 pupils. Practically, however, it is difficult to organize the schedule of a period so that each gymnasium class will have the same number of pupils. Proportional increases or deductions should be made according to the number of pupils and the number of class periods.

One gymnasium will be adequate where the school enrolls from 200 to 600 pupils. In small schools of fewer than 200 pupils one room might serve as the gymnasium for boys and girls, and also for the town hall. It might also be used for community recreation centre and for public meetings. A room used for combination purposes should have the windows and lights protected with wire screens to avoid breakage during games. The walls and ceiling should be of concrete, metal, or wood rather than plaster, for the same reason. No gymnasium should be constructed less than 50 by 70 feet.

I omit the recommendations about showers and lockers, pools and playgrounds, as the requirements of the different countries, in these matters, must vary.

Under the head of Time Allotment, the committee recommends that "two double periods (each single period of 45 minutes) should be considered a minimum for this work, out of which one period of 45 minutes (twice a week) is allotted to exercises and games, and the rest to the teaching of hygiene, shower bath, dressing and undressing, etc. It is added that these exercise periods of 90 minutes twice per week should be supplemented by play periods after school of at least one hour, and, of course, by the regular recess periods and setting-up exercises between class periods.

The committee then proceeds to give a schedule showing how the 90-minute periods for physical education can be fitted into the regular weekly schedule of the school, and ends as follows :—

This schedule provides for seven classes of 50 pupils each ; that is, theoretically, 350 pupils per day per gymnasium, or 875 different pupils on the basis of two double periods per week for each pupil. This arrangement uses the gymnasium continuously and allows for alternation of two teachers in instruction in hygiene, physical education practice, and supervision of the bathing. Three hours of instruction during the school day, plus two hours on the playground and in the gymnasium or pool after school, should be the maximum requirement for one teacher. The remainder of the day is needed for administration and the keeping up of equipment, records, etc.

The following remarks of the committee on the kind of exercise are too valuable to be omitted :—

(a) *Physiological Type of Exercise.*—The types of exercise used should be those which call into play vigorously the large fundamental groups of the big muscles; these exercises are related to the development of vigour, endurance, and power. This instruction should be supplemented by exercises of skill, grace, and alertness. Special attention should be given to securing good postural habits while standing, sitting, and exercising. The training should give a virile, vigorous body, alert and well poised. Instruction should be given in gymnastics, athletics, swimming, and team games for all pupils.

(b) *Character-building Activities.*—By proper control and administration of the team games and athletic contests undesirable features and excesses of the representative teams can and should be eliminated without stopping games which have great health, social, and moral values when played and conducted in the right way. This is more rational than the radical remedy of abolishing them. Abolishment of the game as a school sport in public schools usually results in the team playing under other than school name and with no regulation. Some of the after-school activities, like the Boy Scouts and Camp Fire Girls, should receive vigorous encouragement.

The curriculum of activity both in school and after school should include all pupils, and should be related not only to health, but to right conduct. The qualities of honesty, fair play, courtesy, cleanness of speech, alertness, promptness, persistency, and manliness should be required of pupils during their activity. Both boys and girls should learn the value of the positive virtues. Dishonesty, unfairness, discourtesy, vulgarity, or profanity should not be tolerated in connection with any activity. Through public and private approbation, teachers, coaches, and the community should honour the pupils of vigour and high ideals, and discipline those who pursue dishonourable tactics.

Teachers and coaches who represent the highest ideals in morals and personal character should be selected. Preferably the coaching should be done by regular teachers, and if possible by the director of physical education. With the adolescent group the basal virtues are *caught* through the inspiring personality of teachers during their direction of activities, more often than they are *taught* through definite moral instruction in the classroom.

Moral instruction shows what is right. Moral action knits together the fibres which form character. Physical activity, particularly team games, rightly conducted, offers great opportunity for moral achievement ; wrongly conducted, the result is moral deterioration. During this adolescent period the vigorous, virile leaders will enter into the team activities. These team boys will, in large measure, influence the moral standards of both the junior and senior high-school groups. The moral standards and personal leadership of the teachers of physical education will be a large factor in determining whether these boys are to be merely healthy animals or future moral leaders in the community. If the " win at any cost " idea dominates the coach, he may be the most potent factor in the community in destroying the moral ideals and the ethical standards of future leaders.

In the opinion of the committee—

the courses in hygiene should receive credit on the same basis as other classroom subjects. The physical practice in gymnastics, athletics, games, and swimming should receive positive credit on the same basis as laboratory courses. The hygiene instruction should be graded on the basis of classroom recitations and examinations. The physical practice should be marked on the basis of the quality of the work, and on the effort of the pupil in daily practice. Tests of minimum physical proficiency should be given at regular intervals.

In summing up, the committee remarks:

The present civilization is making great demands upon the vitality of the race. School practices which train simply eye, ear, tongue, and hand do not promote the health of the pupils. Laboratory work, shop work, military drill, and domestic science only slightly increase the big muscle activity. Big muscle work is essential to the health of the pupils. These activities are not secured in the home or in the street. Big muscle activities are essential to vocational and other kinds of skill. The higher levels of the nervous system depend for stability and health upon the organic development of the middle and lower levels. Big muscle work in the plays and games is an essential part of emotional control in relation to character building. . . .

The programme of activity under competent supervision should secure physical, social, educational, and moral results.

The report does not deal with the primary school and the college, but the principles enunciated here can, with modifications, be applied to these departments also. My object was to draw attention to the importance of the problem and to show how it is being solved in one of the advanced countries of the West. I want my countrymen to realize that the problem of physical education is a national problem of the first magnitude, and they should apply themselves to its solution with all the energy and the force of soul they possess. It is obvious that we in India cannot copy the United States. But surely we can attend to the gradual application of principles and the introduction of measures to enforce them as circumstances and funds permit.

X

AN ALL-INDIA SCHEME AND AN ALL-INDIAN LANGUAGE

THE METHODS OF TEACHING

HAVING considered the broad aims and ideals of our future national educational policy, we are now free to consider the other points included in our programme.

The first of them is the desirability of having an All-India scheme, or a national scheme as distinguished from provincial and local schemes. This can be considered from two different angles:

(1) From the angle of the language and (2) from that of the subjects.

National Language.—It is desirable that we should carefully consider the question of the future national language of India and arrive at some tentative decision. The choice lies between Hindustani and English. The adoption of the latter will be a great hindrance in the speedy dissemination of knowledge, which we earnestly desire. I will dismiss it without any further discussion.

I may assume that the country will readily adopt Hindustani as the future national language of India, if the Hindus and Mussulmans could come to an agreement on the question of script. The adoption of Hindustani as a national language does not in any way affect the provincial vernaculars. The provincial vernaculars must be the medium of instruction in the primary schools of each province, with the addition of Hindustani as an All-India language, the Hindus learning it in Deva Nagri and the Mussulmans in Urdu characters. For the first four years of a child's life, no other language should be thrust upon him.

(2) The subjects of study should include, besides the three R's, (*a*) the teaching of patriotism, (*b*) hygiene, (*c*) drawing, (*d*) geography of India, (*e*) elementary geography of the world, and (*f*) history of India (local and provincial history and geography must, of course, be taught), (*g*) elements of civics, (*h*) music, and (*i*) modelling.

(3) As far as is possible, the same text-books should be used all over India; the local and provincial subjects should be dealt with in local and provincial text-

books. The printing of text-books should be a Government monopoly. All private profiteering from the sale of text-books must be done away with. The text-books should be supplied free in all primary schools, or sold at cost price.

The above suggestion does not imply that all these text-books must be in Hindustani. By no means. They should be in recognized provincial vernaculars and in very easy, simple language.

Every province should recognize its principal vernacular as the medium of instruction. All attempt to impart education in local dialects should be discouraged. It will be disastrous to our national unity to insist that education be imparted through local dialects. Nowhere in the world is that done, and we should look with suspicion at this suggestion from whatever quarter it may come.

The vernaculars, to be adopted as mediums of instruction, should be as few as may be compatible with the educational interests of the children. A certain amount of efficiency will have to be sacrificed at the altars of provincial integrity and national unity. For example, it will be absurd to insist that for primary education of the

Bengalees the different dialectic variations of the spoken language be recognized, or that *Ooriya* be raised to the status of a language; or that in the Agra division of the Upper Provinces, education be imparted in Braj, *Bhasha*; and in other divisions in their divisional dialects; or that in the Multan Division of the Punjab education be imparted in the Multani dialect, and so on.

Next comes the question of the classical languages, and of English and other modern languages of the world. The remarks that I have made about Sanskrit apply with equal force to Arabic and Persian. In my judgment, English should be compulsory in the second half of the elementary school period or, say, in the last three years, taking the elementary school period to be eight years, from five to thirteen.

The object should be to lay the foundations of a working knowledge of the language, as distinguished from its literary side.

The second period of the elementary course should include general elements of modern sciences. The second part of elementary education might have two alternative courses: one for those who want to enter life on the completion of the course, and also those who want to take up higher courses in agriculture, commerce, and technology; and the other for those who intend to pursue a general course of higher liberal education.

English should be compulsory in both courses, but only as a language and not as a medium of instruction. No one who wants to complete his education with the elementary school or to pursue higher courses in agriculture, commerce and technology, should be compelled to study any classical language. He may learn another modern language besides English if he chooses, but his chief concern should be a preparation for life, including an intelligent understanding of the political machinery of the country.

When in India, I often heard a general complaint about the multiplicity of subjects in the school curriculum, resulting in the impairment of the health of the scholars, as well as in making them mere cramming machines. Now, the complaint is well-founded, so far as its effects are concerned, and I am one of those who believe that an education which impairs the health of the recipients thereof is not worth having. But the fault lies not with the subjects or their number, but with the method in which they are taught.

The art of teaching in India takes no cognizance of the individual boy or girl. It is a kind of mechanical process aimed at filling the scholar's mind and body with so many facts and figures. The individual boy or girl is treated as a kind of clay, which the teacher is required to shape after a given pattern, filling it with so much stuff of a particular stereotyped kind. The prevalent idea seems to be that the boys and girls exist for schools and teachers, and not the latter for the former. The teacher cares more for examinations and discipline than for the mind and the body of his students. The aim before him is to finish so many pages within a given time, and to prove to the examiner, whenever he comes, that the boy remembers what he has been taught.

I wonder if there is one among a thousand teachers in India who thinks, or who has been told, that the real purpose of education is to help the child to become a thinking and an acting person. Man is an animal. But he is a thinking animal. The broad aim of education is to help him to become a thinking man. Life is mostly thinking and acting. Reading and writing are only means to enable human beings to bec better thinkers and actors. The filling of memory and discipline form a very minor part of the life of a human being. Yet instruction in schools and colleges in India is mostly made up of the latter. Nay, active steps are taken in most schools and colleges to put down thinking and action. Independence of thought and action is punished, and obedience and cramming are rewarded and admired.

The inspecting officers never fail to record their opinions about the discipline of the school inspected, but they never note whether the teaching was directed toward the development of the faculty of thinking. Doing, of course, is not contemplated by the curriculum of studies at all. Indian schools never take notice of the fact that the eye, the hand, and the mind are meant for other purposes than that of handling the books, reading the printed letter and committing to memory what is taught. Languages are taught in the time-worn, old, discarded way. Indian boys are expected, one and all, to know the old masters of the English language. Examinations are conducted with the single eye to see what good, correct and idiomatic English the boy writes.

Numerous boys are prevented from pursuing any higher course, be it in medicine, commerce, or mining, or engineering or any other department of industrial and technical knowledge, because they fail to satisfy the examiner in what is known as paper B in the matriculation examination of the Punjab University, i.e. translation from vernacular into English.

A boy who aims to become a Sanskrit scholar, or a Persian scholar, or an Arabic scholar, must also satisfy the examiner to the same extent as one who aims to work for the master's degree in English language and literature. In fact, the education imparted is generally unrelated to the chief work of the boy's life.

Complaints of this kind as to the principles and methods of teaching are quite common, even in such advanced countries like Great Britain and the United States of America. The system in operation in India, however, is about fifty years behind that of other countries ; and we shall have to make enormous efforts to bring it up to the level of what is already being done in other countries. The task is one of educating the instructors and the educators ; of creating public opinion and of enforcing its decisions.

At this stage I think it will be useful to refer to the opinions of two representative writers on the subject; one an English scholar and the other an American. Says Bertrand Russell :—

> Education is, as a rule, the strongest force on the side of what exists and against fundamental change: threatened institutions, while they are still powerful, possess themselves of the educational machine, and instil a respect for their own excellence into the malleable minds of the young. Reformers retort by trying to oust their opponents from their position of vantage. The children themselves are not considered by either party; they are merely so much material, to be recruited into one army or the other. If the children themselves were considered, education would not aim at making them belong to this party or that, but at enabling them to choose intelligently between the parties; it would aim at making them able to think, not at making them think what their teachers think. Education as a political weapon could not exist if we respected the rights of children. If we respected the rights of children, we should educate them so as to give them the knowledge and the mental habits required for forming independent opinions; but education as a political institution endeavours to form habits and to circumscribe knowledge in such a way as to make one set of opinions inevitable.

On the constructive side, Bertrand Russell again remarks :—

Education is essentially constructive, and requires some positive conception of what constitutes a good life. And although liberty is to be respected in education as much as is compatible with instruction, and although a very great deal more liberty than is customary can be allowed without loss to instruction, yet it is clear that some departure from complete liberty is unavoidable if children are to be taught anything, except in the case of unusually intelligent children who are kept isolated from more normal companions. This is one reason for the great responsibility which rests upon teachers: the children must, necessarily, be more or less at the mercy of their elders, and cannot make themselves the guardians of their own interests. Authority in education is to some extent unavoidable, and those who educate have to find a way of exercising authority in accordance with the *spirit* of liberty.

Where authority is unavoidable, what is needed is *reverence*. A man who is to educate really well, and is to make the young grow and develop into their full stature, must be filled through and through with the spirit of reverence. It is reverence towards others that is lacking in those who advocate machine-made cast-iron systems : militarism, capitalism, Fabian scientific organization, and all the other prisons into which reformers and reactionaries try to force the human spirit. In education, with its codes of rules emanating from a Government office, its large classes and fixed curriculum and overworked teachers, its determination to produce a dead level of glib mediocrity, the lack of reverence for the child is all but universal. Reverence requires imagination and vital warmth ; it requires most imagination in respect of those who have least actual achievement or power. The child is weak and superficially foolish, the teacher is strong, and in an every-day sense wiser than the child. The teacher without reverence, or the bureaucrat without reverence, easily despises the child for these outward inferiorities. He thinks it is his duty to "mould" the child: in imagination he is the potter with the clay. And so he gives to the child some unnatural shape, which hardens with age, producing strains and spiritual dissatisfactions, out of which grow cruelty and envy, and the belief that others must be compelled to undergo the same distortions.

The man who has reverence will not think it his duty to "mould" the young. He feels in all that lives, but especially in human beings and most of all in children, something sacred, indefinable, unlimited, something individual and strangely precious, the growing principle of life, an embodied fragment of the dumb striving of the world.

Mr. Bertrand Russell then proceeds to point out how public education is used by the States and the churches *for the maintenance of the existing order*, or, at the most, where the individual is considered, how it is restricted to the idea of "making money" or the art of "getting on" or "achieving a good position."

Russell feels, as all do, that some of the things which education achieves at present must continue to be achieved in the ordinary way, in all civilized countries; as, for example, the preliminary knowledge of the three R's. The actual instruction in these subjects, as given now, may be inadequate, but it is not positively harmful. "It is in history and religion and other controversial subjects" that it "is positively harmful. These subjects touch the interests by which schools are maintained; and the interests maintain the schools in order that certain views on these subjects may be instilled. History, in every country, is so taught as to magnify that country; children learn to believe that their own country has always been in the right and almost always victorious, that it has produced almost all the great men, and that it is in all respects superior to all other countries. Since these beliefs are flattering, they are easily absorbed, and hardly ever dislodged from instinct by later knowledge."

To take a simple and almost trivial example: the facts about the battle of Waterloo are known in great detail and with minute accuracy; but the facts as taught in elementary schools will be widely different in England, France, and Germany. The ordinary English boy imagines that the Prussians played hardly any part; the ordinary German boy imagines that Wellington was practically defeated when the day was retrieved by Blucher's gallantry. If the facts were taught accurately in both countries, national pride would not be fostered to the same extent, neither nation would feel so certain of victory in the event of war, and the willingness to fight would be diminished. It is this result which has to be prevented. Every State wishes to promote national pride, and is conscious that this cannot be done by unbiased history. The defenceless children are taught by distortions and suppressions and suggestions. The false ideas as to the history of the world which are taught in the various countries are of a kind which encourages strife and serves to keep alive a bigoted nationalism.

Speaking of the evils of "good form," he observes :—

The evils of "good form" arise from two sources: its perfect assurance of its own rightness, and its belief that correct manners are more to be desired than intellect, or artistic creation, or vital energy, or any of the other sources of progress in the world. *Perfect assurance, by itself, is enough to destroy all mental progress in those who have it.* And when it is combined with contempt for the angularities and awkwardnesses that are almost invariably associated with great mental power, it becomes a source of destruction to all who come in contact with it. "Good form" is itself dead and incapable of growth; and by its attitude to those who are without it, it spreads its own death to many who might otherwise have life.

Of course he does not mean that "bad form" and bad manners are virtues; what he says is that undue emphasis on "good form" of a particular kind is narrowing and restricting.

On the evils of teaching religion, he is even more emphatic :—

> The prevention of free inquiry is unavoidable so long as the purpose of education is *to produce belief rather than thought, to compel the young to hold positive opinions on doubtful matters rather than to let them see the doubtfulness, and be encouraged to independence of mind.* Education ought to foster the wish for truth, not the conviction that some particular creed is the truth.

About obedience and discipline :—

> Certain mental habits are commonly instilled by those who are engaged in educating: *obedience and discipline, ruthlessness in the struggle for worldly success, contempt towards opposing groups, and an unquestioning credulity, a passive acceptance of the teacher's wisdom.* All these habits are against life. Instead of obedience and discipline, we ought to aim at preserving independence and impulse. Instead of ruthlessness, education should try to develop justice in thought. Instead of contempt, it ought to instil reverence, and the attempt at understanding; towards the opinions of others it ought to produce, not necessarily acquiescence, but only such opposition as is combined with imaginative apprehension and a clear realization

of the grounds for opposition. Instead of credulity, the object should be to stimulate constructive doubt, the love of mental adventure, the sense of worlds to conquer by enterprise and boldness in thought. Contentment with the *status quo*, and subordination of the individual pupil to political aims, owing to the indifference to the things of the mind, are the immediate causes of these evils; but beneath these causes there is one more fundamental, the fact that education is treated as a means of acquiring power over the pupil, not as a means of nourishing his own growth. It is in this that lack of reverence shows itself; and it is only by reverence that a fundamental reform can be effected.

. . . What is to be desired is the free choice of ends with which it is not necessary to interfere.

Discipline, as it exists in schools, is very largely an evil. There is a kind of discipline which is necessary to almost all achievement, and which perhaps is not sufficiently valued by those who react against the purely external discipline of traditional methods. The desirable kind of discipline is the kind that comes from within, which consists in the power of pursuing a distant object steadily, foregoing and suffering many things on the way. This involves the subordination of impulse to will, the power of a directing action by large creative desires even at moments when they are not vividly alive. Without this, no serious ambition, good or bad, can be realized, no consistent purpose can dominate. This kind of discipline is very necessary, but can only result from strong desires for ends not immediately attainable, and can only be produced by education if education fosters such desires, which it seldom does at present.

Such discipline springs from one's own will, not from outside authority. It is not this kind which is sought in most schools, and it is not this kind which seems to me an evil.

He sums up his ideas on fear of thought in this manner :—

Men fear thought as they fear nothing else on earth—more than ruin, more even than death. Thought is subservient and revolutionary, destructive and terrible ; thought is merciless to privilege, established institutions, and comfortable habits ; thought is anarchic and lawless, indifferent to authority, careless of the well-tried wisdom of the ages. Thought looks into the pit of hell and is not afraid. It sees man, a feeble speck, surrounded by unfathomable depths of silence ; yet it bears itself proudly, as unmoved as if it were lord of the universe. Thought is great and swift and free, the light of the world, and the chief glory of man.

But if thought is to become the possession of many, not the privilege of the few, we must have done with fear. It is fear that holds men back—fear lest their cherished beliefs should prove delusions, fear lest the institutions by which they live should prove harmful, fear lest they themselves should prove less worthy of respect than they have supposed themselves to be. " Should the working-man think freely about property ? Then what will become of us, the rich ? Should young men and young women think freely about sex ? Then what will become of morality ? Should soldiers think freely about war ? Then what will become of military discipline ?

Away with thought! Back into the shades of prejudice, lest property, morals, and war should be endangered! Better that man should be stupid, slothful, and oppressive than that their thoughts should be free. For if their thoughts were free they might not think as they do. And at all costs this disaster must be averted." So the opponents of thought argue in the unconscious depths of their souls. And so they act in their churches, their schools, and their universities.

No institution inspired by fear can further life. Hope, not fear, is the creative principle in human affairs. . . . The wish to preserve the past rather than the hope of creating the future dominates the minds of those who control the teaching of the young. . . . Education should not aim at a passive awareness of dead facts, but at an activity directed towards the world that our efforts are to create. It should be inspired, not by a regretful hankering after the extinct beauties of Greece and the Renaissance, but by a shining vision of the society that is to be, of the triumphs that thought will achieve in the time to come, and of the ever-widening horizon of man's survey over the universe. Those who are taught in this spirit will be filled with life and hope and joy, able to bear their part in bringing to mankind a future less sombre than the past, with faith in the glory that human effort can create.

I have given these long extracts in order to show how one of the foremost English thinkers of the age, a man typical of what is best in English thought, feels in this matter. The reader also must think independently and not accept his opinions as gospel truth. That there is a great deal of truth in what he says cannot be denied.

The American writer whose thoughts on education I wish to commend to my readers, is Professor John Dewey, of Columbia University, New York. His book, "Democracy in Education," of which I will quote some paragraphs in the next chapter, is verily a classic on the subject.

XI

VOCATIONAL EDUCATION

THE Indian people are poor, miserably poor. When we say that, we do not speak of the Indian landlord or the capitalist, nor of the Indian lawyer or the merchant, nor even of the stock exchange broker or the high salaried Government servant, but of the Indian ryot and the Indian working-man, of the petty trader and the petty landowner, of the petty Government servant and the poor artisan and craftsman. Everybody knows it, and even the highest among the Anglo-Indian administration do not question it. Yet India is a country rich in the productive power of its soil, in minerals, in human as well as material resources. Before the British occupied the country, the people did occasionally suffer from famines, which sometimes took a very heavy toll of human life, but in ordinary times the people had plenty to eat and could easily meet the other demands of life.

Their standards of life were simple, as compared with countries of colder climate; the wages were low, but the necessities of life were cheap and could be had without much trouble. Some idea of the standard of wages and the prices that prevailed in the time of Akbar, in the second half of the eighteenth century, can be had from the details left in the Áin-i-Akbari, which have been quoted at some length by Mr. Vincent Smith in his Life of Akbar, published by the Oxford University Press.

Moreover, the gulf between wealth, competence and poverty was not as wide as now. The economic life of the world has since then undergone a revolution. The invention of the power engine and the introduction of machinery has completely changed the economic conditions of the world. The standard of life has been raised considerably, and with it wages as well as prices. Countries that availed themselves of the steam power and the machine have amassed untold wealth at the cost of others who, either by ignorance or for lack of freedom, could not use machinery.

Before the advent of machines for the production of commodities, mankind lived in what is called the Pastoral Age. The chief occupation of men in each country was to produce food, and the greater bulk of the population engaged themselves in that business. Comparatively few people pursued handicrafts and indulged in art. Yet art played a great and an agreeable part in industries. People liked to make good things and took pleasure in creating beauty. The tools of agriculture were more or less antiquated, and much depended on traditional knowledge acquired by apprenticeship in the fields. Similarly the other necessities of life were also produced by hand and with the help of hand tools.

People were not pressed for time and they did their work leisurely. The industries were not capitalized, in the modern sense, and most of the work was done by individual craftsmen in their homes and shops on their own initiative.

The craftsmen organized themselves into guilds, and were completely independent of capital in the management of their respective imdustries. Each industry stood by itself, taking its place in the economic life of the nation, without that subservience to capital, to storing, distributing and transporting agencies which characterize modern life.

People had plenty of time to think of things other than material, and gave a free rein to their fancies and imagination. We express no opinion as to whether they were happier than their descendants under modern conditions are. The economic life of the nation moulded the national system of education. Roughly speaking education had two sides, religious or secular—or in modern terms, cultural and economic, though in strict logic it is difficult to justify this classification. Religious or cultural education was in charge of priests and monks—Brahmins or Bhikshus in India and China, Moulavees and Mullas in Western Asia. Secular education in handicrafts or arts was imparted at home or in shops, by a long apprenticeship.

With the British assuming the government of India, the economic life of the country changed. Agriculture or the production of food and raw materials still remained the principal occupation of the native, but the handicrafts and industrial arts gradually perished for want of patronage. The importation of cheap machine-made articles killed these industries. The men who thus lost their means of livelihood also took to agriculture.

The administration has done a great deal to extend the area of agriculture by providing artificial means of irrigation and by making large tracts of waste land available for cultivation. A network of railways has been built to enable the cultivator to sell his produce at the best prices possible, and to purchase articles of dress and comfort made in other countries almost at his door. With the dying out of handicrafts and arts, the education by apprenticeship was no longer needed. The educational institutions of the country did not cater to instruction in modern industries or modern methods and by modern tools. Thus the only economic stimulus to education was either Government service or the learned professions. Men engaged in trade still received their training by the old, time-honoured method, i.e., by apprenticeship in the shop.

In the meantime the educational systems of the world have been revolutionized by the economic needs of the age. Not only industries and trades, but even agricultural methods have undergone a colossal transformation. Everything has been vivified by the touch of scientific knowledge, systematized, standardized, and organized on a scientific basis. Where one ear of corn was produced before, scientific cultivation produces ten now. Similarly the quality and the size of various products have been universally improved. The standard of living has been raised and the needs of men multiplied. Production has been facilitated, increased and improved by the use of machinery and by the adoption of other scientific measures. Thus the world has gone ahead, while we have lagged behind. This is no place to fix responsibility and to indulge in recrimination. The situation is gruesome and dark. The poverty of our masses is a fact that pursues us like a ghost, in everything we do and undertake. The economic helplessness of the younger generation is tragic. Their anxiety to live a better life, economically as well as culturally, meets with pathetic failure. The waste of human and natural resources that results therefrom is colossal. We carry on our foreheads the mark of inferiority and antiquation. Economic helplessness demoralizes us politically as well as otherwise. If we are to survive as a nation, we have to do something to remedy this state of things and to do it quickly. Even Mr. Austen Chamberlain, our late Secretary of State, in a moment of exalted statesmanship, said that India must develop her industries and that she cannot be allowed to remain "the drawer of water and the hewer of wood" for the rest of the Empire.

The war has proved that the industrial inefficiency of India is a great danger from both defensive and offensive points of view. So it is no longer a question of comfort or luxury or of wealth and poverty, but one of life or death. We must devise a system of education which will fit the future generations of India for the battle of life on modern lines. Some good people do not look with approval on modern industrial life. From a spiritual and cultural point of view, there is a great deal in what they say, and the spiritual and cultural point of view is too important and vital to be altogether ignored. After all, there is a great deal of truth in the saying that food and drink do not constitute all of life. No, it is not all of life, but without it there is no life. If we are to live, we must have it, and if it can be had only at fixed price, we must pay that fixed price. We should be failing in our duty if we do not put forth the best in us, to find a solution, which would enable us to have enough food and drink without losing our soul. But to sit silent, for fear lest in our attempt to get the former we lose the latter, is not only unmanly, but suicidal. We shall save neither. We shall simply die, and die perhaps never to be re-born.

Vocational Education—its meaning. The remedy is a widespread system of vocational education. Now the expression, vocational education, has, in the mouth of some people, acquired a bad odour, so that in the language of Professor Dewey, "it is necessary to define the meaning of vocation with some fulness in order to avoid the impression that an education which centres about it is narrowly practical, if not merely pecuniary. A vocation means nothing but such a direction of life activities as renders them perceptibly significant to a person, because of the consequences they accomplish, and also useful to his associates. Professor Dewey, in his "Democracy and Education," says:—

> We must avoid not only limitation of conception of vocation to the occupations where immediately tangible commodities are produced, but also the notion that vocations are distributed in an exclusive way, one and only one to each person. Such restricted specialism is impossible; nothing could be more absurd than to try to educate individuals

with an eye to only one line of activity. In the first place, each individual has of necessity a variety of callings, in each of which he should be intelligently effective; and in the second place any one occupation loses its meaning and becomes a routine, keeping busy at something in the degree in which it is isolated from other interests. (1) No one is just an artist and nothing else, and in so far as one approximates that condition, he is so much the less developed human being; he is a kind of monstrosity. He must, at some period of his life, be a member of a family; he must have friends and companions; he must either support himself or be supported by others, and thus he has a business career. He is a member of some organized political unit, and so on. We naturally *name* his vocation from that one of the callings which distinguishes him, rather than from those which he has in common with all others. But we should not allow ourselves to be so subject to words as to ignore and virtually deny his other callings when it comes to a consideration of the vocational phases of education. (2) As a man's vocation as artist is but the emphatically specialized phase of his diverse and variegated vocational activities, so his efficiency in it, in the humane sense of efficiency, is determined by its association with other callings. A person must have experience, he must *live*, if his artistry is to be more than a technical accomplishment. He cannot find the subject matter of his artistic activity within his art; this must be an expression of what he suffers and enjoys in other relationships—a thing which depends in turn upon the alertness and sympathy of his interests. What is true of an artist is true of any other special calling.

There is doubtless—in general accord with the principle of habit—a tendency for every distinctive vocation to become too dominant, too exclusive and absorbing in its specialized aspect. This means emphasis upon skill or technical method at the expense of meaning. Hence it is not the business of education to foster this tendency, but rather to safeguard against it, so that the scientific inquirer shall not be merely the scientist, the teacher merely the pedagogue, the clergyman merely one who wears the cloth, and so on.

The Place of Vocational Aims in Education.—(*a*) It is of vital importance to everyone, first to find out what he is fitted to do, and then "to secure an opportunity to do it." This, says Professor Dewey, is "the key to happiness."

Nothing is more tragic (he adds) than failure to discover one's true business in life, or to find that one has drifted or been forced by circumstances into an uncongenial calling. A right occupation means simply that the aptitudes of a person are in adequate play, working with the minimum of friction and the maximum of satisfaction. With reference to other members of a community this adequacy of action signifies, of course, that they are getting the best service the person can render.

(*b*) The only adequate training for an occupation is the training *through* occupation, and as "an occupation is a continuous activity having a purpose," education *through* occupation combines within itself more of the factors conducive to learning than any other method.

Yet there are dangers against which provision requires to be made in giving training *for* occupation, *through* occupation. A very early determination of the occupation for which a person is to be trained, might injure the possibilities of present development and thereby reduce the adequacy of preparation for a future right employment. Such a course might lead to technical efficiency, but otherwise hamper the individual's development both intellectually and morally. Consequently, it is suggested that "all the earlier preparation for vocations be indirect rather than direct." Again, Professor Dewey says :—

> The only alternative is that all the earlier preparation for vocations be indirect rather than direct ; namely, through engaging in those active occupations which are indicated by the needs and interests of the pupil at the time. Only in this way can there be on the part of the educator and of the one educated a genuine discovery of personal aptitudes so that the proper choice of a specialized pursuit in later life may be indicated. Moreover, the discovery of capacity and aptitude will be a *constant* process as long as growth

continues. It is a conventional and arbitrary view which assumes that discovery of the work to be chosen for adult life is made once for all at some particular date. One has discovered in himself, say, an interest, intellectual and social, in the things which have to do with engineering, and has decided to make that his calling. At most, this only blocks out in outline the field in which further growth is to be directed. It is a sort of rough sketch-map for use in direction of further activities. It is the discovery of a profession in the sense in which Columbus discovered America when he touched its shores. Further explorations of an indefinitely more detailed and extensive sort remain to be made. When educators conceive vocational guidance as something which leads up to a definitive, irretrievable, and complete choice, both education and the chosen vocation are likely to be rigid, hampering further growth. In so far, the calling chosen will be such as to leave the person concerned in a permanently subordinate position, executing the intelligence of others who have a calling which permits more flexible play and readjustment. And while ordinary usages of language may not justify terming a flexible attitude of readjustment a choice of a new and further calling, it is such in effect. If even adults have to be on the lookout to see that their calling does not shut down on them and fossilize them, educators must certainly be careful that the vocational preparation of youth is such as to engage them in a continuous reorganization of aims and methods.

Comparing the older methods of vocational education through apprenticeship with its limited scope and tendency towards establishing the superiority of the purely intellectual, literary or administrative pursuits over those involving manual labour, Professor Dewey proceeds to the cause, for the present, of conscious emphasis on vocational education.

In the first place, there is an increased esteem, in democratic communities, of whatever has to do with manual labour, commercial occupations, and the rendering of tangible services to society. In theory, men and women are now expected to do something in return for their support—intellectual and economic—by society. Labour is extolled; service is a much-lauded moral ideal. While there is still much admiration and envy of those who can pursue lives of idle conspicuous display, better moral sentiment condemns such lives. Social responsibility for the use of time and personal capacity is more generally recognized than it used to be.

In the second place, those vocations which are specifically industrial have gained tremendously in importance in the last century and a half. Manufacturing and commerce are no longer domestic and local, and consequently more or less incidental, but are world-wide. They engage the best energies of an increasingly large number of persons. The manufacturer, banker, and captain of industry have practically displaced a hereditary landed gentry as the immediate directors of social affairs. *The* problem of social readjustment is openly industrial, having to do with the relations of capital and labour. The great increase in the social importance of conspicuous industrial processes has inevitably brought to the front questions having to do with the relationship of schooling to industrial life. No such vast social readjustment could occur without offering a challenge to an education inherited from different social conditions, and without putting up to education new problems.

In the third place, there is the fact already repeatedly mentioned : industry has ceased to be essentially an empirical, rule-of-thumb procedure, handed down by custom. Its technique is now technological; that is to say, based upon machinery resulting from discoveries in mathematics, physics, chemistry, bacteriology, etc. The economic revolution has stimulated science by setting problems for solution, by producing greater intellectual respect for mechanical appliances. And industry received back payment from science with compound interest. As a consequence, industrial occupations have infinitely greater intellectual content and infinitely larger cultural possibilities than they used to possess. The demand for such education as will acquaint workers with the scientific and social bases and bearings of their pursuits becomes imperative, since those who are without it inevitably sink to the rôle of appendages to the machines they operate. Under the old regime all workers in a craft were approximately equals in their knowledge and outlook. Personal knowledge and ingenuity were developed within at least a narrow range, because work was done with tools under the direct command of the worker. Now the operator has to adjust himself to his machine instead of his tools to his own purposes. While the intellectual *possibilities* of industry have multiplied, industrial conditions tend to make industry, for great masses, less of an educative resource than it was in the days of hand production for local markets. The burden of realizing the intellectual possibilities inhering in work is thus thrown back on the school.

In the fourth place, the pursuit of knowledge has become, in science, more experimental, less dependent upon literary tradition, and less associated with dialectical methods of reasoning, and with symbols. As a result, the subject matter of industrial occupation presents not only more of the content of science than it used to, but greater opportunity for familiarity with the method by which knowledge is made. The ordinary worker in the factory is of course under too immediate economic pressure to have a chance to produce a knowledge like that of the worker in the laboratory. But in schools, association with machines and industrial processes may be had under conditions where the chief conscious concern of the students is insight. The separation of shop and laboratory, where these conditions are fulfilled, is largely conventional, the laboratory having the advantage of permitting the following up of any intellectual interest a problem may suggest ; the shop the advantage of emphasizing the social bearings of the scientific principle, as well as, with many pupils, of stimulating a livelier interest.

Finally, the advances which have been made in the psychology of learning in general and of childhood in particular fall into line with the increased importance of industry in life. For modern psychology emphasizes the radical importance of primitive unlearned instincts of exploring, experimentation, and "trying on." It reveals that learning is not the work of something ready-made called mind, but that mind itself is an organization of original capacities into activities having significance. As we have already seen, in older pupils work is to educative development of raw native activities what play is for younger pupils. Moreover, the passage from play to work should be gradual, involving not a radical change of attitude but carrying into work the elements of play, plus continuous reorganization in behalf of greater control.

Underneath this emphasis on vocational education, however, lurks a danger that vocational education might be interpreted in theory and practice as trade education, as a means of securing technical efficiency in specialized future pursuits. Education would then become an instrument of perpetuating unchanged the existing industrial order of society, instead of operating as a means of its transformation. It might lead to the perpetuation of the present division of society into manual workers and cultured leisured classes. To avoid this, " an education which acknowledges the full intellectual and social meaning of a vocation would include instruction in the historic background of present conditions; training in science to give intelligence and initiative in dealing with material and agencies of production; and study of economics, civics, and politics, to bring the future worker into touch with the problems of the day and the various methods proposed for its improvement.

XII

THE MONEY VALUE OF EDUCATION

JUDGED from the point of view of national wealth and individual production, India and China are among the poorest countries of the world, perhaps the poorest of all; yet between them they claim very nearly one-half of the whole human race. India, alone, has about one-fifth of humanity residing within its borders.

Racially, physically, intellectually, the Indians are among the highest and the best peoples of the earth. One of the most outspoken critics of Indian civilization, Mr. William Archer, has in his recent book, "India and the Future," remarked that "the Indian races, take them all round, are not low, but *very high races*. . . . The peoples of India stand high among the races of the world. They stand high in stature, proportion, power, dignity, delicacy; and, judged by the highest standards known to us, they often excel in beauty. *Some of the noblest types* of mankind I have ever seen were, or rather are, Indians." (The italics are mine.) True, he makes no mention of their mental capacity, but I hardly think he intended to make any reservation in that respect.

But besides Mr. Archer, we have many other testimonies of the high mental capacity of the Indians as a race. Taking them at the highest, they have produced intellectual giants of which the world may well be proud. Taking them at the lowest, the average Indian is mentally inferior to no average man of any race in the world. In the course of my life and work I have come in contact with Indians of all classes and castes. For the last fifteen years I have been taking special interest in what are considered the lowest classes of the Indian population, the so-called depressed classes. I have met them in my office, in courts, in towns, in villages, at their homes and in their fields. In my judgment, in mental capacity they are not inferior to the highest among us. The average illiterate Indian peasant has, in my opinion, a better mind than the average working man of European and American factories. At any rate, he is in no way inferior to them. Yet we find that his annual income is very much less than that of the latter. His annual production is less in quantity and inferior in quality and brings less money in exchange. The question naturally arises, Why? The answer is, "Because of his lack of education."

We have heard a great deal of the desirability of keeping education free from sordid motives. In season and out of season we have been told that knowledge should not be sought for and judged by its money values; that it should be pursued for its own sake and that to put a money value on education is to degrade it to the lowest level of ordinary material commodities. Knowledge, it is said, is its own reward and an end in itself.

To me it seems that this whole idea is the result of defective thinking. Neither education nor the resultant knowledge can be ends in themselves. They are at best only means to other ends, however unmaterial these ends may be. Knowledge illumines the mind, enlightens the soul, broadens the outlook, leads to elegance, refinement, and culture. It leads to salvation and success. It is a gateway to the abode of bliss, whether here or hereafter.

Yes, all this is true; but, after all, it is

only one of the means to other ends—never an end, itself. Education, as I have said before, is a social function, the transmission of the experience and thoughts of others. Its value depends on its aims and purposes. An education which does not fit its recipient to increase his productivity, thereby adding to his own usefulness, as well as to that of the society of which he is a member, is certainly defective. No person can live on air. Much less can a nation.

The first requisite of an efficient system of national education is that it enable every citizen to live better, and to help others in living better. To live well, one requires a certain minimum of food, clothing, shelter, leisure, recreation, and means for the satisfaction of higher tastes and higher cravings. A nation which does not secure enough to enable every one of its members to live well, is a drag on the rest of the world. But when a nation of 315 millions of human beings, as well developed as the Indians, in possession of a country so rich in soil as that of India, with abundant natural resources of all kinds, cannot produce sufficient to satisfy even the minimum demands of half of its population, it is a sight for the gods to weep at. India's phenomenal poverty is one of the tragic facts of its life; and it is mainly due to the lack of means of education.

Under the circumstances, the first aim of all publicly imparted education in India should be to increase the productive capacity of its citizens. Education is the first necessity of such a nation, and it should be the first charge on all national revenues. The nation should strive with every nerve to deprive itself of all *luxuries*, nay, even of secondary necessities, in order to place this first necessity of national life within the reach of every boy and girl, and of every adult capable of learning. This is only possible by a general widespread system of vocational education, and by a general dissemination of practical, scientific knowledge applicable to the ordinary needs of life and vocational efficiency.

Such a widespread system of education requires huge funds. These funds are to be furnished (*a*) by existing revenues, (*b*) by new taxes, (*c*) by economy in other departments of public administration, (*d*) by national or provincial loans. In order to prepare the public mind to meet the demands for funds for education, it is necessary to bring home to the people "the material and measurable rewards of education."

The United States Bureau of Education has tried to do this by their bulletin on the Money Value of Education (No. 22 of 1917), from which we take the following facts and figures. The compiler of this bulletin (Dr. A. Caswell Ellis, Professor of the Philosophy of Education in the University of Texas) has made an almost world-wide investigation of the subject, and gives the results obtained, as regards each country.

GERMANY

The concrete evidence of the effect of education in increasing industrial efficiency is overwhelming, whether considered from the national standpoint or from that of the individual citizen. For example, how else account for the fact that a nation like Germany, with limited natural resources, but with excellent public schools, has grown in wealth and power so much more rapidly than her neighbour, Russia, which has a vigorous and talented national stock and vastly better resources but poor educational facilities? That the phenomenal success of Germany is the direct result of her thorough educational system is generally admitted.

JAPAN AND RUSSIA

Similarly the relation of her school system to the remarkable development of Japan and her proved ability in the highly technical and complicated art of modern warfare is universally admitted. The defeated Kuropatkin states that the costly failures of Russia were due to the ignorance of her brave but untutored army, and to the education of the Japanese. Writing of the causes of defeat, he said: "The non-commissioned officers in the Japanese army were much superior to ours, on account of the better education and greater intellectual development of the Japanese common people. The defects of our soldiers—both regulars and reservists—were the defects of the population as a whole. The peasants were imperfectly developed intellectually, and they made soldiers who had the same failing. The intellectual backwardness of our soldiers was a great disadvantage to us, because war now requires far more intelligence and initiative, on the part of the soldier, than ever before. Our men fought heroically in compact masses, or in fairly close formation, but if deprived of their officers they were more likely to fall back than to advance. In the mass we had immense strength, but few of our soldiers were capable of fighting intelligently as individuals. In this respect the Japanese were much superior to us. . . . Among many of the common soldiers whom we took as prisoners we found diaries which showed not only good education, but knowledge of what was happening and intelligent comprehension of the military problems to be solved."

THE UNITED STATES AND OTHER COUNTRIES

The remarkable results in these instances cannot be attributed to racial or climatic differences, for in like manner, in Denmark, in Scotland, in Switzerland, in Massachusetts, wherever there is adequate provision for education, there follow great industrial efficiency and national wealth.

On the other hand, in Spain, in Russia, in Turkey, in Mexico, wherever there is a lack of the necessary school system, there is the same story of poverty, revolution, and misery, regardless of race, climate, or abundance of natural resources. Even in the United States it has been shown that the earning capacities of the citizens of several States are in direct proportion to the efficiency of their school systems. Dr. Charles W. Dabney, who investigated this matter, found, for example, that the average schooling given in 1898–9 to the citizens of Massachusetts was 7 years; to those of the United States as a whole, 4·4 years; while that of Tennessee was only 3 years. Corresponding to these figures, he found that the average daily production of the citizen of Massachusetts was 85 cents; that of the United States as a whole was 55 cents; while that of Tennessee was only 38 cents.

Other concrete illustrations of this fact are at hand. For example, Mullhall[1] gives the annual earning capacity of the inhabitants of several European countries as follows:

NATIONS WITH EFFICIENT EDUCATIONAL SYSTEMS.		NATIONS WITH INADEQUATE EDUCATIONAL SYSTEMS.	
England	£36	Spain	£16
France	31	Greece	13
Germany	25	Russia	10

[1] "Industries and Wealth of Nations," pp. 391 and 393, published in 1896.

The effect of education upon the accumulation of wealth is equally notable. The figures given by Mullhall for the total wealth per inhabitant of these several European nations are :

NATIONS WITH EFFICIENT EDUCATIONAL SYSTEMS.		NATIONS WITH INADEQUATE EDUCATIONAL SYSTEMS.	
England	£302	Spain	£135
France	252	Greece	101
Germany	156	Russia	61

Similarly in America, Massachusetts, with slightly smaller population than Texas, has $4,956,000,000 of accumulated wealth to $2,836,000,000 possessed by Texas.[1] That this is not altogether due to the fact that Massachusetts is a much older State than Texas is shown by the fact that Wisconsin, a comparatively new State, with only about two-thirds the population of Texas, has an equal amount of wealth ; and California, a newer State, with only two-thirds the population, has $4,115,000,000 of wealth. All three of these richer States for years spent two or three times as much per child on education as Texas spent.

The relation of productive power to education is shown by the enormously increased rate of production that has come about everywhere since education became more generally diffused. The total wealth accumulated in America from 1492 to 1860, a period of 368 years, was $514 per capita. From then till 1904, a period of only 44 years, this increased to $1,318 per capita, or an addition in 44 years of $802

[1] All figures are from the Special Report of the Census Office on Wealth, Debt, and Taxation, 1907, p. 37.

per capita.[1] Since that time the increase has been even more striking. This increase is partly due to increased valuations or the smaller purchasing power of the dollar; to the use of accumulated capital, and to many other things; but after due allowance is made for all these the conclusion is inevitable that the education of the Nation is largely responsible for vastly increasing the productive power of its citizens. The productive power of illiterate countries is not increasing at such rates.

Why educated nations produce more.—That there must be this intimate relation between education and earning power is obvious as soon as consideration is given to the demands of the processes of modern industry. The Asiatic farmer, with his stick plough, makes 6 cents a day,[2] and the illiterate Russian

---

[1] Figures from the Special Report of the Census Bureau on Wealth, Debt, and Taxation, 1907, p. 9.

[2] "Report on Taxation, Proceedings and Addresses," Nat. Educ. Assoc., July 1905, pp. 27–8:

"In India only 5 per cent. can read and write, and there the men receive for farm work, in the Madras district, 6 to 8 cents a day; women, 4 to 6 cents; children, 3 to 5, the labourers boarding themselves" (pp. 6 and 16).

"If Asia had a Panama Canal to dig, she would dig it with picks, hoes, and spades, and tote out the earth in buckets. Nothing but human bone and sinew would be employed, and the men would be paid little, because without tools and knowledge they must always earn little. But America puts brains, science, steam, electricity, machinery into her Big Ditch—tools and knowledge, in other words, and she

peasant with his primitive implements and methods earns 14 cents, while the American farmer earns many times these sums because his improved methods and implements, made possible by education, have increased his efficiency. The illiterate race is necessarily restricted to the bullock and the stick plough, while the educated nation mines and smelts ores, manufactures the reaper and the traction engine, fertilizes the soil, rotates crops, breeds better stock and better seeds by scientific methods, rises superior to flood, drought, and disease, and multiplies efficiency a hundredfold.

Natural resources worthless without education.—Even a bounteous harvest in a fertile section would avail little for an illiterate people who could not build the engines or boats to transport it, or understand the processes necessary for its preservation against a future day of want. Without the knowledge of chemistry and metallurgy, rich mineral deposits are but so much worthless rock. Without tools and machinery and educated skill to turn them into houses, furniture, and implements for man, vast timber resources are but so many trees cumbering the soil. Without educated brain and skilled hands, the fertile soil, timbered land, water power, and mineral deposit must for ever lie idle or be ignorantly squandered.

Comparison of illiterate and educated workers.—Horace Mann vividly pictures the power of education

---

pays good wages because a man thus equipped does the work of ten men whose only force is the force of muscle." "Asia's Greatest Lesson for the South," Clarence H. Poe, pp. 10–11.

in his statement about the savage and transportation. Modifying his statement, it can be said: The savage can fasten only a dozen pounds on his back and swim the river. When he is educated enough to make an axe, fell a tree, and build a raft, he can carry many times a dozen pounds. As soon as he learns to rip logs into boards and build a boat, he multiplies his power a hundredfold; and when to this he adds mathematics, chemistry, physics, and other modern sciences he can produce the monster steel leviathans that defy wind, storm, and distance, and bear to the uttermost parts of the earth burdens a millionfold greater than the uneducated savage could carry across the narrow river.

The efficiency of an illiterate people in competition with an educated nation is as the crooked stick against the sulky plough; the sickle against the reaper; the bullock cart against the express train, the ocean greyhound, and the aeroplane; the pony messenger against the telegraph, telephone, and wireless; the individual harangue against the printing press, the newspaper, the library; the spinning wheel against the factory; the pine fagot against the electric light; the peddling of skins and herbs from the oxcart against the bank, the cheque book, the railroad, the department store; the log hut against the steel skyscraper; the unaided eye against the microscope and telescope; incantations and magic against the chemist, the hospital, the modern physician and surgeon. Take away from one entire generation all education, and society must revert to the stick plough, the oxcart, and such primitive means, because steel implements, locomotives, steamships, electricity, telephones, telegraph, waterworks, steel buildings, mining and chemical industries, factories, modern sanitation, hygiene and medicine, books, newspapers, courts of justice, and laws that protect property and defend the rights of the weak are all impossible without education, and are efficient only in proportion as educated intelligence is applied to them.[1]

The necessity for education rapidly increasing.—The necessity for education has increased and will continue to increase with the advance in the complexity of the processes of civilization. Because of the unparalleled progress in the arts and sciences during the past fifty years the need for education has in a generation multiplied many fold. For example,

---

[1] The advantage to each of the education of all is admirably brought out in the following paragraph from Mr. Clarence Poe: "You prosper just in proportion to the prosperity of the average man with whom you are brought into business contact. If the masses of the people are poor and ignorant, every individual, every interest, every industry in the community will feel and register the pulling-down power of their backwardness as inevitably as the thermometer records the temperature of the air. The merchant will have poorer trade, the doctor and lawyer smaller fees, the railroad diminished traffic, the banks smaller deposits, the preacher and teacher smaller salaries, and so on. Every man who through ignorance, lack of training, or by reason of any other hindering cause, is producing or earning only half as much as he ought, by his inefficiency is making everybody else in the community poorer." ("Asia's Greatest Lesson for the South," Clarence H. Poe, pp. 3-4.)

a century ago a transportation system was little more than a wagon and a driver who knew the road. Now, in handling a problem of transportation, experts in traffic must first determine whether a road in that place will be worth while, and what kind of road will be most economical and efficient; experts in finance must provide the tremendous sums needed to build the road; civil engineers must lay it out; bridge engineers plan the bridges; chemical engineers test the materials; mills and factories with scores of chemical and physical experts make the rails, build the locomotives and steel cars; and a host of traffic experts, auditors, accountants, and specially trained managers and clerks, telegraphers, engineers, conductors, and others keep the trains moving with safety and with profit. In like manner the farmer can no longer merely exhaust one fertile piece of fresh soil after another by crude methods of agriculture. Intelligent rotation must be planned, soil must be conserved and built up, improved stock and seed must be bred; methods of cultivation that stimulate growth and conserve moisture and fertility must be practised; markets must be studied and considered in planting; new methods of marketing must be used, accounts must be kept, and homes must be made healthful. If this is not done the landowner will soon lose his land and become a tenant, and the tenant become a day labourer. In law, in medicine, in teaching, in manufacturing, in trade and industry of all kinds, this same increased demand for education is found.

A banker's opinion.—Speaking in 1905 at Girard College, Mr. Vanderlip said:

"The mental equipment of a business man needs

to be greater to-day than was ever before necessary. Just as the sphere of the business man's actions has broadened with the advent of rapid transportation, telegraphs, cables, and telephones, so have the needs of broad understanding of sound principles increased. It was steam processes of transportation and production that really made technical education necessary. The electric dynamo created the demand for educated electrical engineers. So the railroad, the fast steamship, the electric current in the telephone and cable, and the great economic fact of gigantic and far-reaching business combinations are making the science of business a different thing from any conception of commerce which could have been had when Girard was the most successful of business men. The enlarged scope of business is demanding better trained men, who understand principles. New forces have made large scale production, and we need men who can comprehend the relation of that production in the world of markets. There has been introduced such complexity into modern business and such a high degree of specialization that the young man who begins without the foundation of an exceptional training is in danger of remaining a mere clerk or bookkeeper. Commercial and industrial affairs are conducted on so large a scale that the neophyte has little chance to learn broadly, either by observation or experience. He is put at a single task; the more expert he becomes at it the more likely it is that he will be kept at it, unless he has had a training in his youth which has fitted him to comprehend in some measure the relation of his task to those which others are doing.

Business growing more complicated.—An excellent

illustration of the manner in which modern business has widened the scope of its demands for training and broad education is given by J. T. Young in speaking of several modern industries : [1]

The production of oil has led to an especially interesting series of auxiliary enterprises. Crude and refined oils, petroleum jelly, gas, gasoline, and light oils, fine and heavy lubrication oils, wax, paraffin, chewing-gum, oil-cake, barrels, tin cans, bags, and wooden boxes are all manufactured in the various departments and plants of the industry. In addition, it has proved profitable to own and operate banks, steamship lines, and various other commercial undertakings.

In gas manufacture, tar, briquettes, light oils, dyes, creosote, and coke are resultant by-products leading to the development of new markets and new departments of business. The most successful meat-packing concerns have been directed by men who are able to develop extensive "allied" industries. Besides the usual dressed fresh, canned, dried, and smoked meats, the packing interests manufacture soups, meat extracts, sausage, lard, toilet, laundry, and wool soap, gelatine, pepsin, glue, fertilizer, etc., and operate printing establishments, can, box, and paint factories, extensive refrigerator car lines, and meat, fruit, and vegetable refrigerating plants. In addition to the manufacturing side of the business, a wholesale organization has been built up which distributes some of the products throughout practically the entire domestic market.

---

[1] Annals Amer. Acad. Pol. and Soc. Sci. 28, pp. 28–37, "Business and Science," by J. T. Young.

The manager of a modern business enterprise of any size must be able to trace the exact cost of production of each article, study the markets of the world in order to make wise contracts for sale and purchase, must know how to advertise economically and create or increase his market, must be able to organize and reorganize the departments of his plant, borrow money advantageously, secure favourable transportation rates, stop wastes, work up by-products, and do many other things that were unknown a few years ago. Without the wide use of former waste products, few large enterprises could now maintain themselves. Indeed, so carefully have these been studied that the by-products are at times the chief source of profit, in some cases modern science turning what was formerly a source of trouble and expense into one of great revenue, as was the case in the turning of the injurious sulphur fumes given off in smelting into sulphuric acid. The Tennessee Copper Co., of Copper Hill, Tenn., several years ago was sued for heavy damages by owners of neighbouring land because the sulphurous fumes given off by the plant did great injury to the trees and other vegetation around. The expert chemist was called in, and he, by his superior education, was able not merely to stop the injury to the vegetation, but to convert these sulphurous fumes into sulphuric acid, one of the profitable by-products of the smelter.

Education and Individual Success.

Who's who in America.—That national wealth and industry are dependent primarily on education and must in the nature of things become more and more dependent thereupon as civilization advances is now so obvious that further illustration is unnecessary. That individual education is an equally vital factor in individual efficiency and success in the varied walks of practical life is a matter about which the facts are not so obvious, as the occasional large successes of comparatively unschooled men and the not infrequent failures of men of much schooling have attracted disproportionate attention and obscured the more significant facts. But in recent years several studies have been made which show the influence of education upon individual success.

An investigation of the educational advantages enjoyed by the eight thousand persons mentioned in "Who's Who in America," for the years 1899–1900, brought out the following facts:[1] Out of the nearly five million uneducated men and women in America, only 31 have been sufficiently successful in any kind of work to obtain a place among the 8,000 leaders catalogued in this book. Out of thirty-three million people with as much as a common-school education, 808 were able to win a place in the list, while out of only two million with high-school training, 1,245 have manifested this marked efficiency, and out of one million with college or university

---

1 "Who Are the Eight Thousand?" a study by W. W. Smith, chancellor of the Randolph-Macon system. Similar statistics given in "Who's Who in America," p. xix, for 1910–11, and covering 15,794 notable Americans, show results "nearly identical" with those for 1899–1900.

training, 5,768 have merited this distinction. That is to say, only one child in one hundred and fifty thousand has been able in America, without education, to become a notable factor in the progress of his State, while the children with common-school education have, in proportion to numbers, accomplished this 4 times as often, those with high-school education 87 times as often, and those with college training 800 times as often. If this list had been selected by the universities or school-teachers, or if literary leaders only were chosen, it might easily be claimed that the apparently greater success of the educated was due to the line of work from which the leaders were selected. But the selection of the men and women in this book was not in the hands of professors, but in the hands of a firm of business men. They selected leaders in all lines of industry, commerce, agriculture, and other fields of practical endeavour besides the professions, and still this enormously increased efficiency and productivity of those with education was found.

In interpreting the results of this study, as in the interpretation of all of the following comparative studies of those who have education with those who do not have it, let it be understood that the remarkable superiority of the educated must not be attributed entirely to their education. Those who receive education are a selected lot to begin with. Their parents were, as a rule, persons of more than average efficiency, and hence were able to keep their children in school; they were more intelligent than the average, and therefore induced or required their children to remain in school. The child himself probably had more than average ability, else he would have wearied of the intellectual labour of the school and would have left it early. Then, too, the child of educated and well-to-do parents has more opportunity offered him to enter lucrative positions. Other influences also doubtless modify the result; but after due allowance for all these factors is made there remains still a large margin of superior efficiency on the part of the educated that one must credit to education or do violence to common sense in interpretation of the undisputed facts.

Financial Return of Education to the Individual.

Individual salary and value to society.—The financial returns which different grades of education make to the individual have been studied recently by two different methods. In some of the studies the investigators went into the factories and other enterprises and found out the amount of schooling that the successful employees in the several grades of work had had. In others they followed out into life the graduates of certain schools and colleges to see what kinds of positions they proved competent to fill, and what salaries they received from year to year. The salary paid to an individual because of certain educational qualifications possessed by him represents not only the financial value of that education to him, but also in a general way represents the financial value which the community places upon the service made possible by that education. Some of the results are as follows:

Dodge's study.—One of the earliest of these studies was made by Mr. James M. Dodge, one of the prominent manufacturers of America and former president of the American Society of Mechanical Engineers.[1] Mr. Dodge calculated the financial value of different grades of education by comparing the earning capacities of common labourers, shop-apprentice trained men, trade-school graduates, and technical-school graduates who were employed in the several large factories under his observation. He capitalized at 5 per cent. the average annual earnings of 50 weeks of work of a member of each of these classes, and took this sum as the potential value of each when making his comparisons. He concludes:

"A chart thus obtained shows that the labourer starts with $3 a week when he is 16, and rises to $10.20 by the time he is 21, but he rises no higher. His potential value at that wage is $10,200. The apprentice or shop-trained worker starts with the same wages as the labourer at 16, but rises more rapidly, and is earning by the time he is 24 years old $15.80. His potential value at that time is $15,800, but he makes no further rise. The trade-school graduate, starting at the same point, rises still more rapidly, and is earning when he is 25 years of age $22 per week, his potential value at this point being $22,000. From this point his wages rise less rapidly, reaching possibly $25 per week at the age of 32, and representing a potential value of $25,000. The graduate of the technical school starts at the same point of a weekly salary of $3, and is earning $4 when he enters college at 18. Upon graduating

[1] "The Money Value of Technical Training," J. M. Dodge, in Transactions of Amer. Soc. of Mechan. Engineers, vol. XXV.

from college at the age of 22 he can draw a salary of $13 per week. He has then already passed the labourer, but is still a little below the shop-trained apprentice. He passes the latter, however, during his first year of employment, but is still below the trade-school graduate, whom he does not overtake until his twenty-fifth year. From this point on he rapidly leaves behind the other three workers, and at the age of 32 is drawing $43 a week, his potential value being $43,000. Thus, four years' training at a technical school makes a man, by the time he is 32, four times as valuable as the labourer, approximately three times as valuable as the shop-trained apprentice, and 72 per cent. more valuable than the trade-school graduate—surely a good return for four years spent in preparation."

Mr. Dodge found that even in the lowest grades of factory work the uneducated labourer was often unsuccessful. Only 35 per cent. of the unskilled remained in the factory even in unskilled work, 5 per cent. went somewhat higher, while 40 per cent. had to be dismissed and 20 per cent. left of their own accord for one cause or another.

Wages of the trained and untrained.—An illuminating comparison was made by Florence Marshall of the wages received by girls in those occupations demanding no training and those that do demand it.

Education and salaries in New York City.—A committee of the Brooklyn Teachers' Association investigated the salaries received by graduates of the elementary schools and by others who stopped school before graduation. Of 192 boys from the elementary schools taken at random, the committee was able to trace 166 till they were about 30 years of age. At that time the average income of these 166 boys was $1,253.05, whereas the average salary of the illiterate worker in Brooklyn was $500 per year. If the parents of these 166 boys had bought each of them an annuity equal to the extra $753 per year, which his education enabled him to earn, it would have cost over $15,000 per boy. As the salaries of these boys will rise considerably after they are 30, while those of the illiterate labourers will not, it is obvious that this elementary education was worth more than a $15,000 capital safely invested for each boy.

Of 1,600 pupils in the night schools this committee found that wages were being received by them as follows:

WAGES RECEIVED BY 1,600 PUPILS IN NEW YORK CITY NIGHT SCHOOLS.

Grade on Leaving School.	Average Age at leaving School.	Average Age at present.	Average Wages now.	Number Years have Worked.
Below 8B	13·3	18·8	$469	5·4
Below 8A	14·1	18·4	424	3·6
First-year high school ..	15·0	17·0	435	2·0
Second-year high school ..	15·6	14·0	466	2·4
Third-year high school ..	15·9	18·0	503	2·1

From the above table it is seen that the pupils who remained through the high school were already, at the end of two years, receiving more salary than those who quit at the eighth grade were receiving after more than five years' work. This is especially significant, as these pupils who left at the eighth grade showed that they were pupils of more than average energy and ambition, in that they, five years after leaving school, were still attending night school trying to improve themselves. Their comparatively slow rise in salary is therefore not to be accounted for by laziness or stupidity, though this may with justice be used to account for some part of the inability to succeed usually shown by the illiterate as compared with school graduates.

This same committee compared the earnings of the children who left school at 14 years of age with those of the children who remained until they were 18 years old.

At 25 years of age, the boy who had remained in school till he was 18 had received about $2,000 more salary than the boy who left at 14, and was then receiving over $900 per year more. From this time on the salary of the better educated boy will rise still more rapidly. However, reckoning the average difference in salary at only $900 per year, this equals an annuity that would cost $19,000 if bought from a reliable insurance company—not a bad return for four years of youth devoted to the school.

The committee of Brooklyn teachers also looked into the schedule of salaries paid for various kinds of work which demanded different grades of education. In 2,394 bakery establishments employing 12,000 males over 18 years of age, but requiring only the most elementary education, the average salary paid was $657 per year, whereas in the city departments demanding education equal to that given by a commercial high school the average salary of 1,579 employees was $1,597. In the bridge department of

New York City the average pay of 130 men, with an average service of nine years, in work demanding no education beyond reading and writing and a little arithmetic, was $982 per year. In the clerical positions demanding the equal of a commercial high-school education the average salary of 31 persons with an average service of 13 years was $1,720 per year. In the engineering department, where high-school graduation and three or four years of college or technical school education were demanded, the average salary of 134 persons with an average service of 7 years was $2,400 per year.

Every day at school worth nine dollars.—The Springfield and Brooklyn studies represent a fair average of what may be expected as a result of a good school system. The increase above $1,000 in salary of later years will more than compensate for the first few years in which the salary is below this figure. The life expectancy of the average high-school boy is more than 40 years. If we take this average annual salary of $1,000 for a period of 40 years and compare it with the illiterate labourer's salary of $500 per year for the same length of time, we can see how richly the child and the community are repaid for each day the child attends school.

$1,000 for 40 years equals	..	$40,000
$500 for 40 years equals	..	20,000
Difference	.. ..	20,000

Twelve years of 180 days each, or a total of 2,160 days of school, bring the child, therefore, an added life income of $20,000, or a return of between nine and ten dollars for each day spent in school.

Education and farm income in New York.—Warren and Livermore, of Cornell, made a study of 1,303 farmers in four townships of Tompkins County, N.Y. They found that no college graduate had been reduced to the position of a renter, and that only 17 per cent. of the renters had more than the district-school education. The average labour income was as follows:

	Per Year.
Of 1,007 with district-school education	$318
Of 280 with high-school education ..	622
Of 16 with college education	847

Of those with high-school education, 20 per cent. were making over $1,000 per year, while only 5 per cent. of those with district-school education were making that much.

In making these selections, we have omitted all statistics about the incomes of University graduates, as well as such in which capital and land, etc., played an important part in the development of education.

The conclusions about individual incomes may sometimes be open to criticism, but the fact that education is the best investment that a parent can make for his children, and a nation for its citizens, is irresistible. Education alone fits a nation for normal, healthy, vigorous life, such as enables it to occupy a position of self-respect and honour among the peoples of the world. An ignorant nation is a helpless, inefficient, unhealthy parasite, at the mercy of every clever, ambitious individual or group of individuals.

XIII

THE CO-OPERATIVE SYSTEM OF EDUCATION

EDUCATORS all over the world are constantly endeavouring to make educational institutions a part of real life; efforts are being made to bridge the chasm which has heretofore existed between the school or college and the ordinary affairs of the world. In the past—and in many countries to-day—educational institutions confined themselves to theory and let practice take care of itself; this has led to severe criticism by practical business men, of college graduates.

A plan, which has been a growth of a number of years, has provided this much-desired means of uniting theory with practice; this plan is set forth in detail in a recent bulletin entitled "The Co-operative System of Education" (Bulletin 37), issued by the Department of Education of the United States. The bulletin treats of a plan of education which has been in operation for a number of years in the engineering department of the University of Cincinnati, one of the big universities in the United States.

By "co-operative system" is meant, according to the bulletin :—

> The co-ordination of theoretical and practical training in a progressive educational programme. Since the agency which furnishes the practical experience is always some branch of actual industry, the reciprocal relation between school and shop permits the fullest possible utilization for educational purposes, of equipment used in commercial production. . . . From the employer's point of view, the most important elements of the co-operative plan are: First, the selection of workers; and, second, the awakening of an enlightened interest in their work through co-ordinated instruction.
>
> From the standpoint of the school and the student, the most important feature of co-operative education is the *realization* of theory through its practical applications. In a very literal sense the studies in the curriculum become "applied subjects." In the use of the word "co-operative," emphasis is placed not only on the kind of training given, but also on the relation between school and industry, and on the method of bringing them together.

The University of Cincinnati considered every educational aspect of the co-operative plan. Its practical application to local industries—Cincinnati is a large manufacturing city—was taken up with local manufacturers, with a view to entering into agreements with firms for the employment of electrical and mechanical engineering students. Of the one hundred firms which responded and co-operated with the University, the following list will give a good idea of the variety of experience offered students: four railroads, a traction company, a telephone company, a gas and electric company, rolling mills, structural ironworks, consulting engineers, city, county, and Federal engineering departments, excavation and building contractors, and manufacturers of machine tools, automobiles, elevators, engines, bicycles and motorcycles, cash registers, fire engines, printing machinery, paper-making machinery, adding machines, roofing, ink, and soap.

As first tried, the following quotation states the details of the course :—

At the beginning, the co-operative course extended over a period of six years, including alternate weeks at the university and in the shop for each school year, and a three-months' period of full-time shopwork (excepting two weeks' vacation) during the summer. Each man had an alternate; so that the shopwork was continued by students of one section while those of the other section were in school. Under this arrangement, the theoretical instruction given in the regular four-year course was combined with the practical experience of a newly devised shop-apprentice course. Theory and practice were carefully graded and co-ordinated, and the student's work was so planned as to familiarize him, first with the simpler, and later with the more complex problems of the plant in which he was employed. For example, in the course in electrical engineering, the first year's work was in the foundry; the next year and a half in the machine shop; the next two years in the commutator, controller, winding, erecting, and testing departments; and the remaining time in the drafting rooms. On the contract, which was signed in triplicate by the student, the firm, and the university, was a blank space to be filled in with the amount and character of the apprentice work. The details of shop and business experience were left to the dean and the head of a given department on the one hand, and the superintendent of the factory on the other.

This plan was followed for four years, at the end of which time the experiment was fully vindicated.

It had shown itself to be adaptable to a variety of courses, including civil, chemical, and metallurgical engineering, and to a range of industries from railroad construction to ink manufacturing. It had survived a panic and the ensuing industrial depression.

But this experimental period had taught many lessons, and changes were made in the co-operative course. The iron-clad contract was abandoned, the only definite arrangement being made was that determining a minimum rate of pay for all entering students ; the terms of the student's employment were so modified as to facilitate his being transferred from one kind of work to another when a change was desirable ; the way was opened for the transfer of a student, though unsuccessful, in one branch of engineering practice, to another department. Business questions were handled through a special agency, and faculty members were left free " to consider primarily the educational value of the various kinds of shop experience. Each of the professors and instructors was assigned a special list of shops and a regular schedule of visiting them."

That theory and practice might be more thoroughly co-ordinated, " there was need for the careful selection and systematic analysis of the various types of work." The six years of nine month periods was shortened to five years of eleven months ; thus not only did the student gain, but the shops did away with " the necessity of providing summer shop work for twice the usual number of men." The weekly alternating scheme was changed to a two-weeks' unit, and this proved a great improvement, as well.

While changes were being made, the curriculum also came under inspection, and the following changes were made :—

> Purely descriptive material . . . was eliminated, in order to secure time for a deeper study of the fundamentals. Overlapping and closely related courses were compared in detail to avoid duplications and omissions. The relation between prerequisite and advanced courses was emphasized, and deficiencies in a student's preparation reported to his instructor in the prerequisite course. Provision . . . was made for the recall of grades in case the student failed to retain a working knowledge of a preparatory subject. The theoretical work of the first three years in all departments . . . agreed as nearly as possible, and specialization . . . was left to the latter part of the course.

Thus it is seen that the co-operative system is itself selective. And, as reorganized, the keynote of the system was adaptability. " In the industries represented by the various co-operating firms there was variety, change, life . . . . ." The co-operative system provided that " the student's practical work should be done amid conditions of actual production. The school planned the courses, shifted the men, and otherwise continued to be the directing head, and in administrative details it adjusted itself to engineering practice."

The report continues :—

> The engineering professors were given full responsibility for the adjustment of shop and school work, and they were relieved of the business details in the relations between students and employers. The commercial part of the work was placed entirely in the hands of a special field secretary in the dean's office. His duties included opening negotiations with new firms, investigating complaints from students or employers, and adjusting wages and working conditions. It was also provided that through the field secretary should be made all promotions, transfers, substitutions of alternates, and other changes affecting the employment of co-operative students.

Lists of co-operating firms, students employed, alternates, etc., was kept in the faculty room. Instructors of the various technical departments visited the shops at regular intervals. The department of co-ordination was developed pedagogically, and it ultimately became a clearing house " for the practical application of engineering theory and for the shop records of individual students. These records, kept on cards designed for the purpose, are filled out every two weeks, and a graphical summary of the data from the card is made each semester." Thus the student's thoroughness in practical training and collateral instruction is systematically followed.

The bulletin explains that "at the beginning of each school period the student enters on the semester card his experience for the shop period (two weeks) just closed." On sheets marked "Record of Co-operative Work" the records "of each man's semester cards are compiled in a statement which, when completed, shows graphically his practical experience for the entire five years. The chief types of work are listed on different sheets, headed M. E., C. E., and so on, for the several departments." A similar record is kept of a man's previous experience and of his wages throughout his university career. The following quotations give a clear idea of the content of the course and of some of the corollary work :—

Instruction sheets.—A later undertaking by the department of co-ordination was an analysis of shop practice and the formulation of a set of instructions for each type of work. Syllabi have been prepared for the principal types of work done by students, and additional sets of instructions are made out from time to time as they are needed.

Since the educational value of a machine or a piece of work is proportional to its complexity, or the amount of thought that has gone into it, the syllabi naturally vary in length and in disciplinary importance. It would be incorrect, however, to assume that the student may profitably spend upon each type of work only the amount of time required to master a set of instructions and problems dealing with a particular machine. It is often found worth while for him to remain longer, in order to become familiar with the arrangement and operation of the department in which his special work is included. Thus, because he can study the surrounding machinery, a student may be justified in operating a drill press longer than would be necessary for him to learn its simple mechanism. In a foundry his training need not be restricted to moulding, core making, and pattern making. From the patterns and castings he will learn much about machine design, and he will naturally receive many ideas concerning foundry management. Timekeeping, inspecting, and other kinds of work which in themselves are comparatively simple may likewise afford such opportunities for observation as to make them very desirable from the standpoint of practical instruction and co-ordination. In all co-ordination outlines, emphasis is placed upon the incidental training which accompanies the various types of work.

Special kinds of work arise from time to time which cannot be anticipated by any syllabus, but which may have greater instructional value than the regular tasks. For example, during the Ohio floods of 1913 some of the students in the civil engineering department suddenly found themselves face to face with problems and respon-

sibilities far beyond their experience. They "made good," *and incidentally learned many important things about railroad construction. At this time a similar opportunity came to the senior class in electrical engineering. The lighting system at Hamilton, Ohio, had been completely disorganized, and much of the equipment had been badly damaged by the flood. The students spent a week in making repairs and, of course, working out the solutions for many practical problems in electrical engineering.*

Inspection trips.—Apart from the varied forms of shop experience, an opportunity to learn by observation is provided by the inspection trips, which are made by all students during the school periods. Student visits to representative engineering industries are carefully planned and graded with reference to the student's course and his progress. During the first year the trips include only the larger and more general phases of industry, and are made under the direction of the department of co-ordination. A typical list of plants visited in the first year is as follows:

1. The Cincinnati Water Works (pumping and filtration plants).
2. The Andrews Steel Co. (rolling mills).
3. The Jarecki Chemical Co. (sulphuric acid, commercial fertilizers, and alum).
4. The Hopple Street Viaduct (under construction).
5. The Cincinnati Milling Machine Co. (machine tools).
6. The Bullock Electrical Co. (electrical machinery).

Each trip is preceded by lectures on the type of plant to be visited, its layout, and its special engineering features. Wherever possible the trip is brought into relation with the student's regular class work. For example, the visit to the Jarecki Chemical Co.'s plant is made in connection with the discussion of the manufacture of sulphuric acid in the class in chemistry. A report of from 5 to 10 pages, including a sketch, is required of each student. All reports are written under the joint direction of the department of English and the technical department concerned. The inspection trips made by upper-class men differ mainly in that they deal with more specific phases of industry, and that they are in charge of the several engineering departments.

Production engineering.—In the last two years of the course, special work is given in production engineering. A study is made of such phases of industry as management, routing of work, cost systems, location, organization, and operation of factories, contracts, specifications, and wage systems. In this course, which is given by the department of co-ordination, the student's experience during the first three years is utilized in giving him standards and methods of management.

While vital changes were being made in the practical side of the course, the theoretical courses underwent an analysis, with the result that much descriptive material was eliminated and more emphasis put upon fundamentals. A part of the curriculum was omitted and new material was introduced to strengthen the important part of the courses. This analysis led to the compilation of valuable data, and a uniform outline was adopted for the presentation of the object, method, and matter of each course.

Work was co-ordinated wherever possible. For instance, written reports and lectures on chemical or engineering or other work served as English composition. This double check upon subject matter and composition resulted in a marked improvement all around. Duplication was avoided. "Omission of certain details, and a change of emphasis on others, constituted the principal features of the reorganization."

One of the valuable changes brought about by the reorganization was the plan making it possible for a student to change from one course to another. For example, the first three years of civil, mechanical, electrical and other engineering courses were made essentially the same in theory; during these three years the student simply studied *engineering*. And he could change from one course to another if he discovered during this period that he was better suited to a different kind of work than that which he had at first chosen. "On the other hand, if he showed sufficient aptitude in one branch of engineering to succeed in three years of practical work, he had earned the right to specialize in the theory of that branch during the past two years of his course."

Investigations were carried on at all times in order to discover the special fitness or aptitude of a student for a particular type of work. The best method, and one which was used most generally, was that of trying a man on the job; this was combined with "an analysis of successes and failures, in terms of the major characteristics of the men and the chief requirements of the job." A failure on a certain piece of work was regarded as significant as a success, and a real experiment was carried out to place men in the work for which they were fitted. This method is crude and unscientific, but in view of the fact that as yet there is no recognized psychological method for dealing with the problem, it was used.

This co-operative plan is not presumed to be perfect, it is not final. Changes must be made to meet changed conditions and demands. But it is a plan which is being adopted more and more in advanced communities. Many secondary schools have adopted it, or some form of it. In high schools where students work in machine shops, factories, foundries, etc., it is being used, and it is recognized that there are great opportunities for using it in agriculture.

Such a plan as the co-operative system in operation in agricultural districts seems to have great possibilities. In one high school in the eastern United States, students are required to do ordinary farm chores, provided they do them intelligently and do a certain amount of reading along with them. Records are also kept of results obtained in the work. In this particular high school, the student has four home tasks for which he is given school credit. Each task consumes a year. "If the student essays to cultivate an acre of ground, the first year, he will be given credit for that if he follows instructions. The next year he may decide to take charge of two, four, or six cows, according to his age. He must do all the work himself and keep detailed records to secure credit at school." His work should also show steady improvement, and an intelligent aptitude for methods of improvement. When the courses are organized according to a systematic plan for the co-ordination of theory and practice, the system has proved of great value to the student, the school and the community.

Requisites for a Successful Co-operative System.

Notwithstanding the many possible applications of the co-operative system, only a few of which have been indicated, it would be a mistake to assume that this type of instruction can easily be put into successful operation in any given combination of circumstances. It will be recalled that the co-operative course was first suggested by the existence, side by side, of an institution for teaching young men, and a great industrial plant in which as graduates these same young men would put their theory into practice. Under the co-operative plan it was proposed merely to take advantage of what may be called the "laboratory of industrial environment" in the training of students whose book learning found practical illustration in that environment. Since one community varies widely from another in the nature and extent of its industrial interests, there must be a corresponding variation in the details of a co-operative course designed to fit a particular community. Thus, the co-operative course in engineering which has been developed at the University of Cincinnati could not be successfully adapted in its entirety by the University of Akron (Akron, Ohio), the University of Pittsburgh (Pittsburgh, Pa.), or the Georgia Institute of Technology (Atlanta, Ga.). Each institution has its own peculiar set of conditions, industrial and educational, and whoever plans a co-operative course must take account of these conditions.

Nor does the adaptation end with designing and establishing the course. Unlike the regular course, which can be administered within a comfortably definite routine, the co-operative system is a perpetual challenge to the vigilance and ingenuity of the executive force. There are, to be sure, no insuperable administrative difficulties, but there are frequent surprises and small adjustments that call for watchful supervision. Still more depends, however, upon the spirit of the teaching staff and of the student body. Although teamwork and a friendly attitude of "give and take" are important in any union of effort, they are vital to the co-operative course; they are, in fact, the essence of co-operation.

XIV

BIBLIOGRAPHY

Prepared by RAM KUMAR KHEMKA

THEORY AND SYSTEMS.

BENNETT, C. W. History of the Philosophy of Pedagogics. 1893.

COOK, H. C. The Play Way; an Essay in Educational Method. 1917.

ELIOT, C. W. Education for Efficiency and the New Definition of the Cultivated Man. 1909.

FERRER, G. The Origin and Ideals of the Modern School. 1913.

FROEBEL, F. The Education of Man. 1900.

GREENE, M. L. Among School Gardens.

HENDERSON, E. A Textbook in the Principles of Education. 1910.

HERBART, J. F. Outlines of the Educational Doctrine. 1909.

HORNE, H. H. The Philosophy of Education. 1905.

JOHNSON, G. E. Education by Play and Games.

JONES, A. J. The Continuation School in the United States. U.S. Bureau of Education, Bulletin No. 1. 1907.

LOCKE, JOHN. Some Thoughts on Education. 1836.

MARK, H. T. Modern Views on Education. 1914.

MOORE, E. C. What is Education? 1915.

MATTHEWS, F. H. The Principles of Intellectual Education. 1910.

MUNROE, J. P. New Demands in Education. 1912.

O'SHEA, M. V. Education as Adjustment. 1908.

PERRY, C. A. Wider Use of the School Plant.

RAYMOND, G. L. Fundamentals in Education, Art and Civics: Essays and Addresses. 1911.

ROSENKRANZ, KARL. The Philosophy of Education. 1907.

ROUSSEAU, JEAN JACQUES. Emile.

SADLER, M. E. Continuation Schools in England and Elsewhere.

SCOTT, WALTER. World Education. 1912.

SHREVES, R. M. The Philosophical Basis of Education. 1918.

SIDIS, BORIS. Philistine and Genius. 1911.

SPENCER, HERBERT. Education—Intellectual, Moral and Physical. 1892.

STEVENS, E. A Guide to the Montessori Method. 1913.

THWING, C. F. Education according to Some Modern Masters. 1916.

YOCUM, A. D. Culture, Discipline and Democracy. 1913.

PSYCHOLOGY OF EDUCATION.

ADAMS, JOHN. The Herbartian Psychology Applied to Education. 1910.

BAGELEY, W. C. The Educative Process. 1906.

BALDWIN, JOSEPH. Psychology Applied to the Art of Teaching. 1895.

BRONNER, A. F. The Psychology of Special Abilities and Disabilities. 1917.

COLVIN, S. S. The Learning Process. 1915.

DE GARMO, CHARLES. Interest and Education. 1902.

DEXTER, T. F. G. and GARLICK, A. H. Psychology in the School. 1902.

HARRIS, W. T. Psychologic Functions of Education. 1908.

HERBART, J. F. Outlines of Educational Doctrine. 1909.

HORNE, H. H. The Psychological Principles of Education. 1907.

KING, IRVING. The Psychology of Child Development. 1903.

LA RUE, D. F. The Science and Art of Teaching.

NEWMANN, ERNST. The Psychology of Learning. 1913.

MUNSTERBERG, HUGO. Psychology and the Teacher.

STERN, WILLIAM. The Psychological Methods of Testing Intelligence.

SULLY, JAMES. The Teacher's Handbook of Psychology. 1897.

THORNDIKE, E. L. Educational Psychology.

EDUCATION—REGIONAL.

ANDERSON, J. T. M. The Education of the New-Canadian. 1918.

BADLEY, J. H. Education After the War. 1917.

FRIEDEL, V. H. The German School as a War Nursery. 1918.

GRAY, H. B. and TURNER, S. Eclipse or Empire. 1916.

HOVRE, FRANS DE. German and English Education ; A Comparative Study. 1917.

JACKSON, CYRIL. Outlines of Education in England.

KING-HARMAN, M. J. British Boys, Their Training and Prospects. 2 vols. 1917.

KLEMM, L. R. European Schools; or What I Saw in the Schools of Germany, France, Austria and Switzerland. 1899.

LAW, N. N. Promotion of Learning in India. 2 vols.

MARTIN, W. A. P. The Chinese, their Education, Philosophy and Letters. 1898.

SCOTT, J. F. Patriots in the Making; What America can learn from France and Germany. 1916.

EDUCATION—SOCIOLOGICAL ASPECTS.

BALDWIN, S. E. The Relation of Education to Citizenship. 1912.

BETTS, G. H. Social Principles of Education. 1913.

BRYANT, V. S. The Public School System in Relation to the Coming Conflict for National Supremacy. 1917.

BUTTERFIELD, K. L. Chapters in Rural Progress.

CARLTON, F. T. Education and Industrial Evolution. 1910.

CHAPIN, F. T. Education and the Mores.

CRONSON, B. Pupil Self-government.

DEAN, A. D. The Worker and the State.

DEWEY, J. Democracy and Education.
How to Think.
Moral Principles in Education.
Schools of To-morrow.
The School and Society.

DUTTON, S. T. Social Phases of Education in the School and Home. 1907.

ELLWOOD, C. A. Sociology and Modern Social Problems.

FERGUSON, CHARLES. The Affirmative Intellect.
The University Militant.
FOUILLEE, A. Education from the National Viewpoint.
GILL, W. K. The School Republic.
A New Citizenship.
GOULD, F. J. Moral Instruction, Its Theory and Practice.
GULLICK, L. H. Popular Recreation and Public Morality.
JENKS, J. W. Citizenship and the School.
JOHNSTON, C. H. The Modern School.
KING, IRVING. Education for Social Efficiency.
KIRKPATRICK, E. A. Fundamentals of Sociology, with Special Emphasis on Community and Educational Problems.
MACKAYE, P. The Civic Theatre.
MATTHEWS, L. K. The Dean of Women.
MORGAN, ALEXANDER. Education and Social Progress.
NEARING, SCOTT. Social Adjustment.
O'SHEA, M. V. Social Development and Education.
RIIS, J. A. Battle with the Slum.
ROBBINS, C. L. The School as a Social Institution.
SCOTT, COLIN. Social Education.
SMITH, W. R. An Introduction to Educational Sociology.
WARD, E. J. The Social Centre.
WARD, W. R. Student Participation in School Government.
WHITE, W. C. and HEATH, L. J. A New Basis for Social Progress.
WOODS, R. A. and KENNEDY, A. J. Handbook of Settlements.

EDUCATION—HISTORY.

BOYD, WILLIAM. From Locke to Montessori; a Critical Account of the Montessori Point of View.

BROWNING, OSCAR. An Introduction to the History of Educational Theories. 1905.

COMPAYRE, GABRIEL. History of Pedagogy. 1905.

CUBBERLEY, E. P. Changing Conceptions of Education. 1909.

DAVIDSON, THOMAS. The Education of the Greek People and Its Influence on Civilization.

DAVIDSON, THOMAS. Aristotle and Ancient Educational Ideals.

GRAVES, F. P. A Student's History of Education. 1915.

HART, J. K. Democracy in Education; a Social Interpretation of the History of Education. 1918.

LAURIE, S. S. Historical Survey of Pre-Christian Education.

MONROE, PAUL. Source Book of the History of Education for the Greek and Roman Period.

MUNROE, J. P. The Educational Ideal; an Outline of its Growth in Modern Times. 1909.

TODD, ARTHUR JAMES. The Primitive Family as an Education Agency. 1913.

TUCKER, L. E. Visualized History of Education; with Two Charts Presenting a General Survey of the Field of Education.

WALDEN, J. W. H. The Universities of Ancient Greece.

WALSH, J. J. Education, How Old the New. 1910.

PRIMARY EDUCATION.

DOPP, K. E. The Place of Industries in Elementary Education.

KEITH, J. A. H. Elementary Education, its Problems and Processes.

ROSMINI-SERBATI, ANTONIO. The Ruling Principles of Method Applied to Education.

SECONDARY EDUCATION.

DE GARMO, CHARLES. Principles of Secondary Education. 2 vols.

JOHNSON, C. H. The Modern High School; its Administration and Extension; with Examples of Interpretations and Significant Movements.

INGLIS, ALEXANDER. Principles of Secondary Education.

MONROE, PAUL. Principles of Secondary Education.

SMITH, F. W. Historical Development of Secondary Education from Pre-historic Times to the Christian Era.

SMITH, F. W. The High Schools; a Study of Origins and Tendencies.

HIGHER EDUCATION.

BOSWELL, F. P. The Aims and Defects of College Education. 1915.

BENNETT, H. M. Women and Work.

MACLEAN, G. E. Studies in Higher Education in England and Scotland. 1917. U.S. Education Bureau, Bulletin No. 16.

NEWMAN, J. H., CARDINAL. The Idea of a University, Defined and Illustrated. 9 vols.

THWING, C. F. Letters from a Father to His Son Entering College.

Letters from a Father to His Daughter Entering College.

VEBLEN, T. Promotion of Higher Learning.

INDUSTRIAL EDUCATION.

BARTON, G. E. Re-education; an Analysis of the Institutional System of the U.S. 1917.

BLOOMFIELD, MEYER. Readings in Vocational Education.

Vocational Guidance.

DAVENPORT, EUGENE. Education for Efficiency. 1910.

DAVIES, J. L. The Workingmen's College.

DAVIS, J. B. Vocational and Moral Guidance.

DEAN, A. D. The Worker and the State; a Study of Education for Industrial Workers. 1910.

KERSCHENSTEINER, G. M. A. The School of the Future; a School of Manual Work.

The Schools and the Nation.

LEAKE, ALBERT H. Industrial Education; its Problems, Methods and Dangers.

MAROT, HELEN. Creative Impulse in Industry. 1918.

LEAVITT, F. M. and BROWN, E. Pre-vocational Education in the Public Schools.

ROBINSON, EMILY. Vocational Education. 1917.

TAYLOR, J. S. A Handbook of Vocational Education. 1914.

BIBLIOGRAPHIES.

BACON, CORINNE. Standard Catalogue, Sociology Section; 1,000 titles of the most representative and useful books in Social, Economic, and Educational Questions. 1918. H. W. Wilson & Co. Standard Catalogue Series.

BIBLIOGRAPHIES on Education Subjects, edited by William H. Burnham; Publications of the Clark University Library, Worcester, Mass. Vols. 4 and 5; Bibliographies prepared by Members of the Seminar in Education at Clark University during the year 1916–17.

CUBBERLEY, E. P. Syllabus of Lectures on the History of Education, with selected Bibliographies and Suggested Readings. 1904.

MACMILLAN CO., New York. Books on Education. 1914.

MONROE, W. S. Bibliography on Education. 1913.

NEW YORK CITY, Education Department, Division of Reference and Research: Teacher's Yearbook of Educational Investigations. 1914. Bulletin 1.

NEW YORK PUBLIC LIBRARY, Circulation Department: Selected books on Technical and Vocational Education. 1913.

U.S. EDUCATION BUREAU: List of References on Vocational Education.

Printed in Great Britain by

UNWIN BROTHERS, LIMITED, THE GRESHAM PRESS, WOKING AND LONDON